THE
LITTLE
BOOK
OF
NEWCASTLE

THE
LITTLE
BOOK
OF
NEWCASTLE

JOHN SADLER & ROSIE SERDIVILLE

The
History
Press

First published 2011
This paperback edition published 2019

The History Press
The Mill, Brimscombe Port
Stroud, Gloucestershire, GL5 2QG
www.thehistorypress.co.uk

British Library Cataloguing in Publication Data.
A catalogue record for this book is available from the British
Library.

ISBN 978 0 7509 9003 5

Typesetting and origination by The History Press
Printed in Great Britain

CONTENTS

ACKNOWLEDGEMENTS

The authors owe a debt of gratitude to the following: staff at Newcastle City Libraries, the Society of Antiquaries Library, North East Centre for Lifelong Learning, Tyne & Wear Archives, Robinson Library, Literary and Philosophical Society, Northumberland Archives, Gateshead Library, Adam Goldwater and Gillian Scott of Tyne and Wear Museums, Colm O'Brien of the North East Centre for Lifelong Learning, Dr Jo Bath for advice on witchcraft and witch-hunters, John Mabbit for his outstanding work on the City Walls of Newcastle, Richard Stevenson for his work on the Great Fire of 1854 and also to Chloe Rodham for the illustrations, another successful collaboration.

INTRODUCTION

Around five decades ago, the city of Newcastle formed a backdrop for the 1970s cult gangster movie *Get Carter*. So successful was Michael Caine's performance as Kray-type henchman Jack Carter that a whole 'Get Carter Heritage' was inspired and begotten. Almost fifty years on and the city looks very different, though the *Get Carter* connection of Gateshead's toweringly squalid 1960s monstrosity of a municipal car park was of sufficient weight to grant numerous stays of execution.

The Little Book of Newcastle is not a full history or gazetteer, but a series of anecdotes drawn from the city's rich history and cultural heritage. What we have tried to do is to give our readers an impression of the place, with all its many quirks and idiosyncracies.

Newcastle has a long and eventful history, from the days of the Romans to the Millennium Bridge, through centuries of bitter warfare, the heyday of coal mining and its status as powerhouse of the industrial revolution. It has its great Norman keep and long stretches of medieval walls, the famous Tyne bridges, a varied cultural, musical and theatrical heritage, ghosts, witches, body-snatchers and rock stars.

Then there's football, of course.

John Sadler & Rosie Serdiville

Oh Newcastle
by Irv Graham

Is there such a place as Eden
Lovely and serene
Oh yes there is my bonny lad
Valley of emerald green
Eden of my father
Newcastle upon the Tyne
Eden of my childhood
Wondrous and sublime
Could there be a spot of heaven
Abandoned by the Gods
Sitting here on earth
To survive against the odds
Look around my bonny lad
Each treasure will be thine
Such it is your heritage
Oh Newcastle upon the Tyne

1

CRIME & PUNISHMENT

RIOTOUS BEHAVIOUR

The year 1740 was a difficult one, more noticeably so for the poor. Harvests were meagre and unscrupulous grain merchants, identified as part of the urban elite and including Mayor Fenwick, were driving prices up by hoarding and profiteering. In barely half a year, prices shot up by a meteoric 160 per cent. By early June the swelling tide of discontent had expanded to riotous proportions. On the 9th of that month, keelmen and miners, acting in concert, helped themselves to the cargo of a grain vessel, a version of the Tyneside Wheat Party. Alderman Ridley was dispatched to negotiate and offered, more in panic than policy, a cap on prices; a bargain he was unable to support having no civic authority to barter on such terms.

As the situation continued to deteriorate and sensing indecision on the part of the wavering corporation, belligerent keelmen, on 26 June, marched towards the Guildhall, a raucous mob at their back. In rising terror, aldermen deployed a body of militia who, bayonets fixed and gleaming, barred the way at Sandhill. Someone fumbled or panicked, a musket flashed and banged, one youthful rioter tumbled lifeless. The protesters surged forward, overrunning the Saturday night soldiers and assailing the Guildhall as though storming the Bastille. The terrified merchants had barricaded themselves in as volleys of stones burst through glass like round-shot and the stout doors finally yielded. No more blood was spilt but the place was thoroughly sacked and the Corporation's cashbox or 'hutch' became an early casualty. Wealth in the not inconsiderable sum of £1,200 was summarily redistributed.

Having failed to resist the mob, the chastened militia were 'escorted' back to their billets, many a felon released from custody and retailers encouraged to sell at the capped prices Ridley had offered. By dusk, however, their ire spent and dissipated through serious lubrication, the rioters dispersed. Next morning, yeomanry from the shires rode through deserted streets, rounding up the few who could be found. These, perhaps forty or so, were unlucky as summary trial and transportation awaited them.

LAW AND DISORDER

For several centuries a rich mercantile clique whose influence was based upon coal monopolies, known as 'Hostmen' (of whom rather more later) dominated civic life at all levels and extended their trade cabals to control the offices of local government. Affinity was the key to influence. Newcastle was a city much directed by an interlocking web of bonds. Circuit judges were entertained liberally by the Corporation as hosts. Relationships worked on several levels, both a web and layer cake. One example was Judge Jeffreys who, no stranger to the delights of cellar and table, was noted for 'drinking to filthy excess till two or three o'clock in the morning, going to bed as drunk as a beast, and rising again with all the symptoms of one who has drunk a cup too much.' To fortify himself for the arduous business of law, the judge continued to imbibe during sessions, allowing his particular brand of gallows humour ample free passage.

Newcastle was perhaps unique in the history of English urban settlement as, for centuries, it remained an outpost. Built as such by Romans, it was to stand in an embattled landscape until 1603, when the Union of the Crowns finally brought the border wars to an end. As a centre for the administration of justice, its gaols were to house some choice rogues, not all of whom accepted their captivity with passivity.

OF GAOLS AND GAOL-BREAKS

Newcastle was blessed with two major gaols for a large span of its history. Until the end of the fourteenth century, the town was under the jurisdiction of the County Sheriff. In the year 1400 Newcastle was awarded a grant of separate county status. Thereafter, the town maintained its own court within the Guildhall and lodged felons in Newgate Barbican. The castle itself and surrounding enceinte remained as part of the wider county process. This was both necessary and inevitable given that Newcastle was an island of urban settlement in a wild frontier landscape. The border wars effectively created a no-mans-land in the upland dales of Northumberland, largely depopulated and then resettled after the Scottish raids unleashed in the wake of Bannockburn in 1314. For over a decade the Scots enjoyed military hegemony, despoiling as far south as York, wasting the shire and levying blackmail from those settlements able to pay.

For just over four centuries the castle in Newcastle remained a gaol; filthy, dark and unsanitary, an echo of squalor and despair is still etched into the bare masonry of the guardroom where most prisoners were housed. One reformer, visiting during the late eighteenth century, criticised the vile conditions and deprecated the practice of showing prisoners like zoo exhibits to the public at 6*d* (2½p) a time. Categories of prisoners were not separated, nor indeed were the sexes with inevitable consequences. A number of the county and town's citizens entered the world in the dread confines of the gaol.

CASTLE KEEP

At few points in its long history could the castle keep ever be defined as offering high security. One of the more notorious escapees was Sir Humphrey Lisle who got away in 1527. This knight had done good service against the Scots but meddled in Scottish border politics, thereby incurring the wrath of the Douglas Regent. Lisle and his son judged it wisest to withdraw to Newcastle to escape but the regent had a long reach and procured their arrest. Most likely both were held in the ancient prison adjoining the Black Gate, traces of which can still be viewed. Both Lisles escaped, with or without the collusion of their guards, joyfully 'trashing' their place of confinement in a burst of furious vandalism. Sir Humphrey went on to develop a new career as a reiver, allying himself with the Armstrongs and Liddesdale riders. He rode once too often, however, and, on his second visit to Newcastle, two years after his escape, fell once again into the hands of the authorities. He was immediately hanged without incarceration.

REBELLIOUS EARLS

When the Rebellion of the Northern Earls erupted in 1569, Newcastle was a frontier bastide in a situation which threatened to degenerate into civil war. The earls were soon corralled, however, by resolute local officers and one of their supporters, a notorious Armstrong rider, 'Jock of the Side', found himself in the keep awaiting execution. Little Jock had enjoyed a career that was both colourful and dramatic even by reiver standards and latterly became the subject of a celebrated border ballad. He could scarcely hope for clemency. Nonetheless, his Liddesdale cohorts had not forgotten him and they staged a daring raid on Newcastle. Like the later, even more famous escape of Kinmont Willie Armstrong from Carlisle, the operation proved a complete success. Jock was sprung and, well-mounted, he and his rescuers spurred northwards in a bid to reach the sanctuary of their own dark glen. Though a posse from the garrison, doubtless humiliated and outraged, spurred after, the Armstrongs made clean away, swimming the Tyne at Chollerford.

> They scarce the other brae had won,
> When twenty men they saw pursue;
> Frae Newcastle toun they had been sent,
> A' English lads baith stout and true
> *Jock O' The Syde*

SHADOW OF THE GALLOWS

Maintenance of law and order was somewhat haphazard during the earlier period, no regular police forces existed and Newcastle was not infrequently a garrison town. Berwick, wrested from the Scots first in 1296 with a vast spillage of blood, would change hands no less than fourteen times until Richard of Gloucester, Shakespeare's 'Crookback Dick', won it back for the final time (to date), nearly 200 years later.

It was not until 1763 that the Town Guard was formed, a rather ad hoc formation, many of whom were former soldiers distinguished by their dark greatcoats and bearing lanterns. Remunerated at the princely rate of half a guinea per week with a full guinea bonus, paid quarterly, their base was the porch of St Nicholas' Church from whence, on the stroke of ten, they set off on nightly patrolling. Theirs was an unenviable task; dank, unsanitary wynds were a rookery of thieves and footpads, though each arrest was worth an extra shilling! Newcastle did not institute a regular police force until 1836; an attempt had been launched four years earlier but foundered in the face of vociferous protests from ratepayers, angered by the costs!

Things were certainly lively enough to justify it. In 1836 the chief constable noted the presence of 71 brothels and 46 houses of ill repute in the city. Action seems to have been inadequate; eighteen years later the number had grown to over 100. Presumably they drew a lot of trade from more than 500 pubs and beer shops. By the 1950s there were 44 of them on Scotswood Road alone.

Newcastle invented the high-speed chase. In 1900 a policeman commandeered a passing car to pursue a drunk on a horse. The car won but it was a close run – they only caught up with the horse a mile later.

The Elswick Riots in 1991 were widely reported nationally. They started when two young men burgling a house in Hugh Gardens were disturbed and climbed up onto a roof. People rampaged through the streets smashing cars, front windows and street furniture. It happened again a decade later: this time the main casualty was a local pub. Oddly enough, local crime writer Martin Waites set his novel *White Riot* in the same area.

OUTLAWS

We nearly had our own wild west. Butch Cassidy's mam was born in Brandling Village. Ann Sinclair Gillies moved to America with her parents when she was a child (that's my mam's maiden name!).

The police box at the top of the Bigg Market was the first in England.

A HANGING MATTER

For many years Newcastle's Town Moor was one of the most popular venues for any decent hanging. Invariably these outwardly sombre occasions were guaranteed crowd-pullers. In 1532 thirty members of the Armstrong affinity, notorious reivers all, were turned off en masse, albeit at the equally popular Westgate gallows. Their severed heads provided a gruesome garnish to the castle's walls. The litany of crimes which merited death was a long one and the Corporation retained the services of an appointed hangman. This was no sinecure, the appointee would be called upon to earn his stipend:

21 August 1752, Richard Brown (keelman) hanged for the murder of his daughter
19 August 1754, Dorothy Catinby hanged for the murder of her illegitimate children
7 August 1758, Alice Williamson (sixty-eight) hanged for burglary
21 August 1776, Andrew McKenzie (soldier) hanged for highway robbery
21 August 1776, Robert Knowles (postman), hanged for opening letters and stealing from them

JANE ('JIN') JAMESON

Hangings combined due solemnity with free festive cheer. As Jane Jameson was led to her execution in 1829, the cavalcade comprised the town sergeants on horseback with coked hats and swords; the town marshal also on horseback in his official costume; the cart with the prisoner sitting on her coffin, guarded on each side by eight free porters with javelins, and ten constables with their staves; then came the mourning coach containing the chaplain, the under sheriff, the gaoler and the clerk of St Andrews. Jane, or 'Jin' as she was commonly known, 'a disgusting and abandoned female of most masculine appearance, generally in a state of half nudity,' sold whatever she could scrounge and, despite her unprepossessing looks, her favours by the Sandgate fountain.

Nor was her temperament calculated to endear. She was addicted to drink, foul-mouthed and fouler-tempered. Both her illegitimate offspring died young. Her mother, an altogether more respectable pensioner, lived in no. 5 the Keelman's Hospital, the nearest thing to sheltered accommodation that nineteenth-century Newcastle had to offer. For some time Jane resided with her mother, also giving house to her current partner, Billy Ellison.

The pair celebrated New Year 1829 in their favoured, gin-soaked manner and, having exhausted their own slender purses, attempted to persuade Jane's mother to fund the ongoing binge. A fearful and protracted row ensued, culminating in Mrs Johnson accusing her daughter of the murder of both her children. Jane, in a paroxysm of drunken rage, seized a poker and drove it spear-like through the old woman. Despite the dreadful wound, Mrs Jameson did not die immediately but survived for several days. Even then, she attempted to divert blame from Jane, alleging she'd fallen onto the poker by accident. Nobody believed her, including the jury at Jin's trial for murder. The verdict was never really in doubt and Jane went to the gallows on 7 March.

GOING OFF IN STYLE

Much imbibing accompanied these popular civic occasions and the accused was expected to play his or her part by treating the crowd to a suitably rousing or witty oration. Highwaymen particularly, as befitted their cavalier trade, could usually be relied upon to go off with aplomb. One Henry Jennings, whose neck was stretched for rustling in August 1786, 'gave an explanation of the cant terms used by robbers and pickpockets etc which he desired to be published for the benefit of the public'.

O'Neil the highwayman, hanged in 1816, was another who met his obligations to an attentive public:

> The cart stopped, and on being drawn under the gallows, O'Neill addressed a few words to his two brothers. He gave one a handkerchief and a watch. He then embraced and took affectionate leave of them. He shook hands with the gaolers and executioner. The cap was drawn over his head and after a few private ejaculations he was suspended. The executioner fulfilled his office well. O'Neil's struggles were short and there was but one evolution of nature.

Once the barber-surgeon pronounced life in the condemned man to be extinct, the corpse was taken by friends and family to be 'waked' at a nearby hostelry before a more solemn interment in St Andrews.

Mark Sherwood was the last man to swing on the Town Moor when, in 1844, he was condemned for murdering his wife.

BAD BEHAVIOUR

For the citizens of Newcastle the town had yet more unseemly pleasures to offer besides public executions. Today's ne'er-do-wells who stagger down the length of the Bigg Market are unwittingly maintaining a long tradition of unruliness and bad behaviour. Only the lighting has markedly improved. As far back as 1745 the *Newcastle Courant* was complaining of 'outrages and disorders lately committed in the Bigg Market' – in this instance some twenty-eight offenders were arrested, four of whom were flogged, one sent to don a red coat and another quartet gaoled. Many a *Journal* reader would no doubt thoroughly approve. As a port and, to all intents and purposes, garrison town, Newcastle offered a range of services. For example, the Quayside was long the haunt of loose women. Writing in the 1820s Aeneas Mckenzie, with suitably Calvinistic disdain, warned his readers of the moral dangers of consorting with those *Cyprian Nymphs* who flaunted their charms so openly on the bustling waterfront and in the maze of narrow chares behind.

Sir Walter Scott offers a pen portrait of the Catholic or 'Recusant' gentry of eighteenth-century Northumberland in *Rob Roy* – the Osbaldistones of Osbaldistone Hall, hard-drinking, hard-riding, swift of temper and as swift to draw steel. In 1752 in the smoky confines of Pinkney's rather notorious Bigg Market Ale House a soldier from General Guise's regiment, Ewan MacDonald, took exception to the anti-Scottish nature of a fellow drinker's ribaldries and, in the brawl, ran him through. This was a busy year for matters of honour – ship surgeon Henry Douglas choked out his life-blood on the Quayside at the conclusion of a sanguinary *duello* with Edward Holliday.

THE MAN WHO SIMPLY WOULDN'T DIE

Even as he mounted the scaffold, however, MacDonald's story was to take a rather sensational twist. At this final moment, the ex-soldier panicked as the noose was placed and, kicking at the hangman, threw him clear from the gallows. Doubtless such inconveniences were something of an occupational hazard and, undeterred, the executioner returned to his task and this time MacDonald was left kicking air. The body, in the usual way, was taken to the Surgeons' Hall for anatomical dissection (see below). Only a single student was in the building and, to his mounting horror, he witnessed the dead man come back to life! This time the hangman, perhaps diverted by his fall, had bungled the job. MacDonald, reviving, began to plead for his life. He was wasting his time as the student calmly bludgeoned him to death – a case of third time *un*lucky. When the student bludgeoner, who had boasted of his swift remedial action, was soon after kicked to death by a skittish horse, some whispered the dead man's spirit had entered the animal!

AN AFFAIR OF HONOUR

One of the most notorious encounters between gentlemen of the better sort took place by the old White Cross on Newgate Street. The 'feid' (feud) or vendetta was a long-established Northumbrian and border custom. John Fenwick of Rock and Ferdinando Forster of Bamburgh were both men of substance, the latter being an MP. Both were guests at a grand jury luncheon held in the Black Horse Inn on Newgate Street. A drink-fuelled altercation followed, each seemingly encouraged by the raucous company. Next morning, when heads should have cleared and blood should have cooled, a chance encounter sparked a resumption of verbal abuse followed by swords. Both men were skilled at arms and for a while the blades bickered and parried without hurt. Forster suddenly lost his balance, slipped and stumbled; his enraged opponent delivered a killing stroke. The White Cross and Black Horse Inn are long gone, though Forster's impressive tomb survives in the chancel of Bamburgh church.

A SURFEIT OF LEAD

In the early hours of a midsummer's morning in 1764, the respectable Mrs Stewart, wife to a pawnbroker, found her slumbers disrupted by the drunken chorusing of Robert Lindsay, keelman and noted reveller who was serenading all Sandgate from their yard wall. The lady ordered the drunkard to be off but he became abusive, her resolute assault with a handy pair of hearth tongs easily rebuffed. Now Mr Stewart was awakened and threatened the garrulous intruder with an unloaded blunderbuss. The couple's first joint attempt at a warning shot proved little more than a flash in the pan, a failure which reduced

Lindsay to paroxysms of laughter. His last, however, for a second shot, blasted in anger, killed him instantly. On 27 August 1764, Stewart paid for ill temper with his life, his name added to the long list of those who danced to the hangman's tune on Town Moor.

THE MYSTERIOUS CASE OF THE SAVINGS BANK MURDER

The work of John Dobson as architect and Richard Grainger as developer changed the face of Newcastle and created the magnificent sweep of Grey Street, acknowledged as one of the finest in Britain. Now destroyed and a bare facsimile hidden away beneath the ghastly pile of Swan House, sits the rump of the Royal Arcade, completed in 1832. Superbly located, as was hoped, adjacent to the likely site of a new main station, this development was quickly snapped up. One of the key lettings was to the prestigious Savings Bank. This initial burst of affluence was short-lived and, with the station now constructed elsewhere, the Royal Arcade went into swift and irreversible decline.

None of this was apparent a mere six years after the grand opening. On 7 December 1838 firemen responded to the alarm when smoke was seen pouring from the building. When they entered nothing could have prepared them for what they saw. Joseph Millie, an employee, reposed in the sack-like indifference of death, his blood and brains garnishing the room. The murder weapon, a bent and spattered poker, lay nearby. The dead man's pockets had been stuffed with paper in an attempt, quite plainly, to remove all traces by fire. The victim was not alone for beside him was the semi-conscious form of Archibald Bolam, a senior figure in the bank.

Bolam's story was a bizarre one. He claimed he had been the recipient of a series of menacing letters, the last of which had arrived at the bank that very day. He averred that this made him fearful for the wellbeing of his housekeeper and he had returned home to warn her. It was thus after hours when he re-entered the bank. He found Millie already dead and was himself suddenly and savagely assaulted by a largely unseen assailant who had then fled, leaving him for dead. His story simply did not hold up, the firemen did not believe he was actually unconscious when they entered; nor did the physical evidence tally.

Over the next few weeks following his arrest on suspicion of murder, investigation revealed Bolam was far from being as respectable as he claimed. His housekeeper was also doubling as live-in mistress and he was a gambler and frequenter of bawdy houses.

While his account of events on the fatal day clearly did not add up, there was little or no motive for a murderous assault upon Joseph Millie. The two were habitually on good terms; there was no sign of embezzlement on Bolam's part. In his summing-up at the trial, the judge directed that at worst he was guilty of manslaughter brought on by some inexplicable fit of murderous madness. Suitably impressed, the jurors returned a manslaughter verdict and Bolam cheated the rope. Rather, he was transported to Australia where the Botanical Gardens in Sydney still features an ornamental sundial gifted by Bolam who had served his time and then prospered. The truth of the case will never be known.

GETTING EVEN WITH THE REVENUE MAN

One of the many entrepreneurs who created what would now be termed 'small and medium-sized enterprises' in the heady Victorian era of expansion was Mark Frater, a former tax-collector who had invested in building up an omnibus company. One of the rising city men, just past fifty years of age he kept an office at no. 2 Blackett Street. On 1 October 1861, a fine autumn morning, the omnibus proprietor paused at the entrance to his office building to chat with a friend. In an instant, this mundane scene was transformed into one of horror.

George Clark who resided, appropriately, close to St Nicholas' churchyard was a failed artisan who had allowed a petty dispute over an unpaid dog licence to escalate. In those days, Frater, as collector, had levied distraint upon Clark's tools. Brooding upon his loss Clark became obsessed with his intended victim. Already of a morose and violent disposition, this obsession soon turned to a murderous rage. On that fateful day, he struck, driving a 5in blade deep into his unsuspecting victim's neck. The mortally wounded Frater was carried into his office where he quickly succumbed to shock and blood loss. Clark was to spend the rest of his days in an asylum for the criminally insane.

MURDER ON THE ALNMOUTH TRAIN

On 18 March 1910, John Innes Nisbet, bookkeeper at Stobswood Colliery near Widdrington, aged forty-four, was found shot dead on the morning train at Alnmouth station. Outside of Agatha Christie novels, railway murders are relatively rare.

The victim, a resident of Heaton, had boarded at Newcastle. His attaché case contained a substantial sum in wages (£370 9s 6d), which he'd been due to pay out. Clearly, then, robbery was not a motive. Police established that the killing must have been committed between Stannington and Morpeth stations, although no murder weapon was found.

The crime became something of an overnight local sensation and the victim's funeral was well-attended. A reward was posted and, three days later, a bookmaker's clerk, Alexander Dickman, was arrested and charged. Evidence against the accused was scanty despite widespread and lurid speculation concerning a supposed relationship between alleged killer and victim. Dickman's subsequent trial and its 'guilty' verdict seemed, to many observers, as resembling something of a travesty. Nonetheless and despite a nationwide appeal for clemency, no appeal was allowed and the convicted man was hanged, still protesting his innocence.

RESURRECTIONISTS

Condemned murderers and criminals whose necks had been stretched upon the gallows were still destined for a measure of civic duty once departed. That is, in terms at least of their mortal remains, for there was a thriving trade in dead flesh. Even notorious cases like Jane Jameson, aged thirty at the date of her execution, provided meat for the dissection table. The Surgeons' Hall, a fine classical edifice, stood aloof from the surrounding squalor of Pandon and Manors, where the carcasses of dead felons such as Jane were displayed for some hours in the courtyard as a ghoulish diversion. After the public had tired of this spectacle the corpse was boiled and flayed to create an anatomical exhibit which eminent practitioners such as John Fife could use as a tool for lecturing. Once the cadaver had been probed and dissected, the remains were simply cremated. Now, of course, we have PowerPoint.

This constant need for anatomical specimens had engendered the pernicious trade of 'resurrectionists'. Nobody on Tyneside quite matched the notoriety which Burke and Hare achieved in Edinburgh, although the pair had spent some time as immigrant labourers in Sunderland where, perhaps, they began their ghastly trade. The Anatomy Act of 1832 was intended to relieve pressure upon medical schools needing a constant supply of recent corpses for teaching and experimentation purposes. The statute provided that any cadaver, remaining unclaimed for 48 hours post mortem, could be properly handed to a medical school.

Prior to this, a decent cadaver might fetch 10 guineas; no mean sum. John Fife was much taken with a local pie-seller, John Cutler, who was physically handicapped. The vendor's anatomical deformity led Fife to offer 10 guineas for dissection rights upon his death. Cutler was not at all offended and readily accepted the offer. The *Newcastle Courant* recorded a funeral in 1826 when the deceased, clearly not greatly mourned, was being carried to his funeral and the mourners, losing interest, found the lure of an ale house more compelling. With only the undertaker and pall bearers remaining in the diminished cortège, the group simply shifted tack to the Surgeons' Hall where the deceased, a miser in life, together with coffin was simply traded on to the dissectors!

A CORPSE TOO SOON

John Fife was not just an eminent medical practitioner but a local politician of radical leanings with links to Chartism, anathema to his more conservatively minded contemporaries. He served twice as mayor and made a virulent enemy of his successor and rival John Carr. On 7 December a certain Mrs Rox died in All Saints' Workhouse. Her relatives, being unlettered, were unaware of the provisions of the Anatomy Act referred to above and assumed, naïvely, that the cost of interment would be borne, as previously, by the parish. Not so of course. No sooner had the time period elapsed than the deceased was whisked off to Surgeons' Hall. The family were outraged. Being devout Catholics, their fury spread like wildfire through the hovels and tenements of Pandon. Mayor John Carr was not normally one to espouse popular unrest – indeed, this was what he detested most in Fife – but his hated rival was, of course, a leading surgeon.

It was Carr, the high Tory, who led a ranting, steaming mob to the gates of Surgeons' Hall (now the Medical School). Carr demanded entry and proceeded to threats when nervous inmates demurred. Thoroughly intimidated, the students unbarred their portal and the mob streamed it. Just in time, the late Mrs Rox was due for 'processing' and her mortal remains snatched from the dissecting table in the very nick of time to be transported in semi-regal state to a lusty wake and finally burial in All Saints'. It is clear nobody had troubled over the fate of this unfortunate woman while she still lived. The magistrates subsequently fined the Medical School, deciding the porters had been a mite overzealous in removing Mrs Rox's body ahead of the statutory deadline; for John Carr, his consorting with the mob provided a neat little win over his radical opponent, Fife.

The iron railings around All Saints' churchyard were not intended purely for decoration. These, and many like them, were erected to deter body-snatchers – resurrectionists. Surgeons were apt to ask few questions if any and 10 guineas proved a significant incentive. Frequently it was more outlying cemeteries which were targeted. In response, metal frames or 'mort-safes' were positioned over fresh burials until sufficient time to allow decomposition to spoil market opportunity had elapsed. So pernicious was the curse of the body-snatchers that some communities erected watch towers and stationed guards over their graveyards.

LEFT LUGGAGE AT THE TURF HOTEL

Prior to the construction of Lloyds' fine new banking hall on Collingwood Street, this was the site of the Turf Hotel, a noted coaching inn, where the York to Edinburgh coaches halted. The booking office provided temporary storage for all manner of goods in transit, some of which might abide there for a period if a connection

was missed. Coaches did not run on Sundays out of deference to
the Sabbath. In September 1825, the clerks were alerted to a rather
nauseous odour apparently emanating from a sealed trunk. This was
destined for a James Syme, whose address was given as no. 6 Forth
Street, Edinburgh. The watch was summoned and a magistrate present
when the chest was rather gingerly opened up. Inside was the body of
a teenage girl, almost certainly one who had died of natural causes and
whose body had been stolen to feed this rapacious medical market. She
was never named and subsequently laid in a paupers' grave.

Distressingly, this proved to be but one of a series of such incidents, and
a further quartet of bodies was intercepted. How many passed though
undetected can only be guessed at. On Christmas Day 1828, the corpse
of a child was discovered and the remains traced to a burial at Whitekirk
near York. The poor little girl had only been interred on Christmas
Eve. Once again the addressee resided in Edinburgh. Over a year later,
on 8 January 1829, a Scot, identified by his accent, stashed another
large trunk in the booking office of the Queen's Head (now Alderman
Fenwick's House) on Pilgrim Street. With suspicions running high, the
box was forced and found to contain the remains of little Lizzie Mills, a
cobbler's child, who had been laid in Ballast Hills Cemetery only a day
or so before. When the grave was examined only very minimal, barely
perceptible, signs of excavation could be discerned.

Only once did one of the resurrectionists, a certain James Aitchison,
come into the hands of the authorities. In November 1828 he was
apprehended, almost literally red-handed, attempting to deposit a
further cadaver-filled trunk at the Turf. Arrested, he claimed to be
a native of Edinburgh and that he was an innocent dupe, paid to
deliver the chest. Surprisingly, he was acquitted for lack of evidence
but, no sooner had 'Mr Aitchison' vanished, than fresh evidence was
unearthed suggesting he had earlier purchased timber to construct the
box. He was never found.

By this time, staff members at the Turf Hotel booking office were
becoming very wary of larger, unclaimed items. One such trunk,
increasingly malodorous, passed back and forwards between
Newcastle and York as nobody was keen to look inside. It is said after
some amount of to-ing and fro-ing the chest, unopened, was simply
dumped into the Tyne.

2

HISTORY – MURDER, MAYHEM & MONEY

A CHIVALRIC AFFAIR

On a hot August day in the year 1388, a Scottish knight, Sir James Douglas, 2nd Earl of Douglas, who, with the Earl of March, had jointly led a picked force of Scottish 'hobilers' or light cavalry down through Northumberland, clashed with Sir Henry Percy, better known as Hotspur. This classic tourney took place in front of one of the extended wooden barbicans (called barriers), erected as additional ad hoc defences in times of strife. For medieval Newcastle such times came around depressingly often.

The reason for the tête-à-tête was that the Percys had been fooled. The Scots they faced were far fewer in number than they had thought, but March was leading a diversionary force only – the main thrust was to strike in the west.

Douglas, the Scottish paladin, could not resist the urge to taunt Percy as the raiders drove northwards after bringing fear and robbery to Durham. Both men were renowned knights and Hotspur was not the sort to ignore a challenge. In view of English garrison and Scottish reivers the two broke lances. This was hugely popular sport; such a duel of champions was expected of warriors of fame and precious honour. It seems Percy got rather the worst of it, losing his guidon or pennon to the Scot who jubilantly bragged he'd ensure this trophy adorned the walls of his fortress at Craigmillar near Edinburgh.

Percy was humiliated, doubly so, for he came to realise he'd been hoodwinked and that the Scots were far weaker in numbers than he'd first feared. This tale of a knightly pennon may be romanticised but Percy did draw out every man he could spare from the garrison, perhaps 5,000 or 6,000, and march north at a forced pace. His troops, mainly mounted on sturdy garrons, covered a full 30 miles during that parched high summer to reach Otterburn by nightfall. Here the Scots, thinking themselves safe, had encamped. A furious, moonlit battle then ensued, with Douglas killed in the fight and Hotspur captured.

> He took a lang spear in his hand,
> Shod with the metal free,
> And for to meet the Douglas there,
> He rode right furiouslie.
> *'Battle of Otterbourne' (Scottish version)*

DRAWING THE BORDER LINE

This murderous fight at Otterburn, glorified in the celebrated 'Ballad of Chevy Chase', was but one of a number of major battles fought by Newcastle and the North against the Scots. This long war, arguably the longest and one of the most ferocious in history, spanned over three centuries. Anglo-Scottish relations had, from time to time, been less than cordial beforehand and, for a while, Northumberland and Newcastle stood at risk of being part of a Greater Scottish Kingdom. We tend to assume that the wide sweep of the Tweed running west to east has always marked the border line, but for centuries this was fluid. Early Anglian kings extended their sway or influence as far north as Perth and made war on both Picts and Scots. It was not until the Battle of Carham, by the Tweed, in 1018 that the emerging northern kingdom pushed the Northumbrians back. The battle was sanguinary, the English clergy suffering very heavy loss as battling clerics sought to hang onto church revenues from the Lothians at all costs. The shade of

Bishop Wilfrid would doubtless have nodded approval, though he was more used to winning.

During the early decades of the Norman period, with the north mercilessly harried by King William who believed obedience could be engendered at sword-point (and, to be fair, he was generally right), the Scots sought to extend their frontier southwards as far as the Tees. The 'New Castle' was subsequently erected to mark a potential frontier. Had this continued, Newcastle and not Berwick would have been the frequent cockpit of the border wars. However, the northerners simply weren't having this; they would not kneel before a Scottish king, even an Anglophile such as David I. Massed beneath St Cuthbert's sacred banner at Northallerton in 1138, the northern knights stood against the might of Scotland's lion and defeated them utterly, King David's wild Galwegians literally bristling with arrows as they fell in satisfyingly large numbers.

Cuddy's flag was to come in handy more than once. It flew over northern English forces at Falkirk in 1298 and Neville's Cross forty-eight years later, and did the business both times. Scottish armies were decimated and, in the latter fight, King David II was captured by a local knight, Sir John Coupland, though not before they'd had a serious set-to and the captor had lost several teeth. This was the making of the up and coming Sir John and the English Crown was suitably grateful. Less so his neighbours who found the upstart so irritating that they eventually murdered him.

A VERY WILD FRONTIER

Newcastle would therefore be a frontier town, the largest in the north – probably rather bigger than its more upmarket neighbour Durham, seat of the omnipotent Prince Bishops. It was the most flamboyant, not to say venal, of these great princes of the church, Anthony Bek, who sold the Barony of Alnwick to Lord Henry Percy in 1313. Bek negotiated the sale in his capacity as trustee on behalf of the de Vesci beneficiaries, although he failed to account for the proceeds which were diverted to fill the Episcopal coffers and never subsequently transferred (a fraud which rankles even today). These Percys became very important in Northumberland and Newcastle's history – at this time the two were very closely interwoven. During the wars of the fourteenth century as successive raids and climatic changes depopulated the upland dales and many a gentleman looked elsewhere for a living, the Percys bought up everything that was going, virtually at clearance prices, while these despoiled and barren uplands were resettled by a harder and purely martial breed.

The Percys would grow into the over-mightiest of over-mighty subjects together with their emerging rivals the Nevilles. Endemic border conflict helped build a power base and northern hegemony that none of the other magnates could boast. Henry Percy (irritatingly and confusingly, they're all called Henry), the 1st Earl, acted as kingmaker, when Henry of Derby unseated his cousin Richard II. The choleric Hotspur, something of an aristocratic thug, fought Glendower in Wales and Scots wherever he could. Finally, they over-reached themselves. The son died a traitor's death at Shrewsbury in 1403, followed five years later by the old fox himself and the Percy star was eclipsed by the Nevilles, whose loyalty saw them elevated to Earls of Westmorland. This was not the end of their rising feud, however. The Percys bounced back and increasing tension between these two rival families sparked a feud that finally blossomed into the Wars of the Roses in 1453.

OUTPOST AND TOWN

450 million years ago, during the Silurian period, Newcastle was well south of the equator, jammed between two continents. A mere 350 million years ago, we were submerged under an ancient sea as our land mass moved slowly northwards.

Newcastle began as a bridgehead, frontier outpost on the northern flank of Rome known as *Pons Aelius*, a line drawn between civilisation, *Romanitas* and the rest. It was a good choice of location. Roman military engineers had a practised eye and the bluff headland dominating the crossing below was ideal for defence. A fort was constructed, much of which lies beneath the great Norman keep – only an outline set in paving stones give us hint as to its extent. At least the Romans built to a standard specification, most obligingly for future generations of archaeologists who can recognise the distinct 'playing card' shape and regular layout of buildings within. Rome left us several legacies including numerous place names: Benwell = *Condercum*, Newcastle = *Pons Aelius*, Tyne = *Tinea*.

NORMAN ENFORCERS

An early Norman keep was thrown up on the site in the late eleventh century, a fairly modest affair to judge by the surviving foundations, hidden beneath one of the railway arches. The New Castle itself came later and remains, loftily massive and mighty, undaunted even now by the overlay of nineteenth-century railway dynamism that pushed by the historic fortress with, by modern standards, breathtaking indifference. Industrial progress, spurred by the heady glow of endless possibility and unlimited capital, had little regard for heritage. The railway distorts our view of the headland, keep and later barbican, known as the Black Gate. Only a careful walk through the traces of the ancient stronghold reveals its strength, land falling dramatically away on the east and south flanks of a triangular spur, with a deep, strong ditch or *fosse* on the west.

Yet another century on from the building of the keep and the full enceinte of town walls was completed. Within these lay much prosperity and a warren of medieval streets linked by a necklace of thoroughfares sprang up, and their pattern is still plain today. The first charter appears to have been granted in 1175 and the appointment of a mayor ordained in 1216 with, as mentioned, county status following by 1400.

It is probable that the early crossings were all built where the Swing Bridge now stands and our understanding of the Quayside is obfuscated by the later structures, the High Level and present Tyne Bridge. The settlement grew from the river bank, with the medieval chares clustering a bustling waterfront. As affluence increased, building moved higher in reach and lower in density with gentlemen's houses gracing the upper levels and suburbs at Sandgate, Newgate, Westgate and Pilgrim Street Gate spreading outwards beyond the impressive bulk of the walls.

FLOWERS OF THE FOREST

The campaign and Battle of Flodden in 1513, perhaps the most dramatic of all in the region, was fought as a consequence of a strategic decision made by Henry VIII of England to invade the realm of France, Scotland's traditional ally, in 1513 in support of his ally, the Habsburg Emperor. This was to prove Newcastle's gravest test until the Civil War well over a century later. James would have done best to stay at home. His army was defeated at Flodden and in a final quixotic gesture, James and his household men flung themselves upon the Earl of Surrey's banners. The King of Scotland died almost unseen in the ruin of his proud army. As dusk fell, the English were masters of the field where perhaps as many as 8,000 Scotsmen fell – the English loss was far less, maybe 1,000 in all. Flodden was the worst of Scotland's many defeats on the English border.

FOR KING OR PARLIAMENT?

When Charles I of England raised his standard at Nottingham in August 1642, few could have foreseen that this quarrel between the king and his parliament would become as bitter and protracted as was to prove the case. William Cavendish, latterly Marquis of Newcastle, held the town (city status was not granted until 1882) and county firmly for the Crown. This was not to say parliament was without supporters, a very influential Presbyterian clique existed. The town, had, however, already had a taste, quite sufficient for most, of Scottish Covenanters two years earlier. For Newcastle, civil war came early, during the second Bishops' War. King Charles had unwisely attempted to ram the Book of Common Prayer, *Laud's Liturgy*, down the throats of his northern subjects who had responded with force of arms.

THE ROUT OF NEWBURN FORD

In August 1640, a large Scottish field army under Alexander Leslie, latterly Earl of Leven, appeared at Newburn, on the Tyne. Lord Conway, with a scratch-built and ill-disciplined force, attempted to bar their passage. The king's men were unruly; some had been shot in Newcastle to stiffen others' resolve. This did not work. The Scots took the fords at Newburn in fine style, although Royalist Cavalry held them off for a spell. However, Conway's forces were routed and the town occupied by Leven's army, a humiliation that even the blackest days of the border wars had not witnessed.

Once the Civil War in England began in deadly earnest, Cavendish moved to secure Newcastle and the north-east, thus providing the king with a first-class port and denying parliament vital coals. Throughout 1642 and 1643 the Marquis enjoyed a virtual hegemony in the north, routing the Yorkshire rebels under the Fairfaxes at Adwalton Moor. Matters changed in strategic terms early in 1644. In miserable deep and drifting snow, a Scottish army, again under Leven, crossed the Tweed that January, as mercenaries in support of parliament.

Cavendish was now on the back foot. He didn't have the men to fight both Scots and Roundheads in the field and many of his officers were themselves Scots, now prone to divided loyalties. He held Newcastle, engaging in a cat and mouse campaign south of the Tyne until both armies moved down to York, where he was besieged. Newcastle remained firmly Royalist but Sunderland changed sides, a defection the larger town found impossible to forgive or forget and it is said the hearty dislike between 'Geordies' (Newcastle) and 'Mackems' (Sunderland) dates from this time. Nobody can claim Tynesiders don't know how to bear a proper grudge.

SIEGE AND STORM

Matters, from the Royalist perspective, took a distinct and irrevocable turn for the worse in July when Newcastle's northern army, together with Prince Rupert's relieving forces, were utterly crushed at Marston Moor. Here the Tyneside Brigade, the Whitecoats (so called on account of the undyed wool of their doublets), were decimated in a hopeless rearguard stance. Of 3,000 who took the field, only 30 survived! Newcastle was doomed, now nothing more than an island of residual Cavalier sentiment in a swelling Parliamentary ocean.

The Scots came north again and this time they settled down to a siege. Sir John Marley, the Royalist mayor, refused to submit, despite no hope of relief. London was still deprived of vital coal supplies and, as autumn drew on, this shortage became increasingly acute. Newcastle's streets and buildings suffered badly from near continuous mauling by Scottish guns; those ancient walls, newly refurbished, were ultimately no match for heavy artillery. Local miners, otherwise idle, were happy to sign up for parliament and dig mines beneath the bruised ramparts. When talks finally foundered, the Scots prepared to storm the battered walls.

A dour Scottish chronicler, William Lithgow, provides a gritty account of the nature of the assault:

> so also I say the breaches of the walls by batteries, being made open and passable, and ladders set to at diverse parts for scalleting [scaling], then entered mainely and manfully all the regiments of our commanded men at all quarters, but more facily [easily] and less dangerous where the mines sprung. The greatest difficulty and mightiest opposition, nay, and the sorest slaughter we received was at the climbing up of these steep and stay breaches, where truly, and too truly, the enemy did more harm with hand grenades than either with musket pike or Herculean clubs. These clubs were anti-personnel weapons devised for just such work, like long, heavy version of a medieval spiked mace it grimly looked like to the pale face of murther [murder].

'Siege and Storm'
– the dead litter the
streets as the Scots
burst through the
defences.

INTO THE BREACHES

Leven's official dispatch, while commendably concise, does provide some greater measure of detail:

> the word was given and the sign made, to give fire to the rest of the mines, and for the regiments to advance all at once towards the breaches, and those places of the wall which were opened by the mine; but he met with no small opposition, and nothing was left undone by the enemy to repel the fury of the assault. They played very hotly and desperately from the castle upon the breaches, and from the flanking towers of the walls with scattered shot; yet the regiments advanced without any shrinking, though the cannon played from many places upon their full open bodies, so that the difficult access to the breaches and the mighty advantages of their walls and works within the town, made a considerable loss of soldiers and officers of good quality.

This was the killing time. As the Scots drew near the rubble-strewn ramps, musket and cannon would contest every step. Grimly, with levelled pikes and clubbed muskets, the attackers pressed on. Those making the assault would be the cream of the army, men who could be relied upon to charge home, regardless of loss. Clearly casualties were high and desperate defenders exacted a fearful toll. As the fight came to 'push of pike', men stumbled and scrambled to come to grips on blood-slicked stone, hacked and clawed at each other, consumed by the adrenalin rush 'red mist' of combat. As the Scots fought their way into Closegate, horse-mounted Royalists tried three desperate charges to push them back, but cavalry could not contest so narrow a space with resolute pikes and regular volleys. From here, as the official account confirms, the attackers 'marched for the relief of the rest of the breaches, and so the soldiers gave over and forsook the walls.'

RECKONING AND AFTERMATH

With the Scots established within the ring of defences, the walls were no longer tenable and men fled back into the streets, apart from those bastions like Newgate and Pilgrim Gate which doggedly maintained their resistance. Surprisingly perhaps the Scots did not then have to fight for possession of a warren of streets and lanes, 'for after their entry, the soldiers did quite vanish, sheltering themselves in houses, the inhabitants kept closed their doors, the regiments marched through the streets without any insolence or disorder.' The Scottish commander was at pains to stress that his men behaved impeccably with a strict avoidance of pillage and offering no violence to citizens not under arms. Once the attackers had breached the ring, bodies of infantry would be told off from the columns to secure the enceinte from within.

Those with fight left in them or who might have had cause to fear retribution had retreated into the castle itself. Leven makes a very clear point that, as the town had refused terms and been taken at sword-point, the Scots were at liberty to sack the place. That they did not reflects well upon standards of discipline. The general does allow that some 'little pillage' did occur, mainly directed against 'some houses of the meaner sort'. Robbing the poor was clearly less reprehensible than pilfering from the rich! Leven goes on to wax lyrical over his own virtue and moderation, and although this rather reeks of pomposity, the citizens had good cause to be grateful. Other towns had fared less well – Continental and Irish sieges conducted in like manner frequently ended in massive bloodshed.

Both town and region were devastated by the war which dragged on until Charles' final defeat in 1646. The king, a 'guest' of his Scottish subjects, spent nine months of his captivity in Newcastle where he was lodged, according to legend, in Anderson Place, a commodious town house which stood where Lloyds' Grey Street branch now stands and a plaque on the wall records the fact. During this time the king played at both golf and politics, he was hopefully, rather better at the first.

Despite the ravages of the Civil Wars, the town fathers felt sufficiently confident to instruct Robert Trollope to build or rebuild the town court and weigh house at the Sandhill in 1655, barely a decade later, evidence of the economic clout of the coal trade. Celia Fiennes found Newcastle possessed 'buildings lofty and large of brick mostly or stone, the streets very broad and handsome.'

THE WHITE COCKADE

Fortiter Defendit Triumphans – 'Triumphing by Brave Defence'. This stirring motto was likely awarded by the restored Charles II after 1660, when Sir John Marley, an exile during the Commonwealth, returned to his former office. By the end of the siege many townsfolk had been baying for his blood, so great were their losses, and indeed much damage had been caused both structurally and economically. However, Tyneside had not quite done with civil war. The 'Glorious Revolution' of 1688 dethroned James II, replaced by his dour son-in-law 'Dutch Billy', William III. Not by any means an attractive character, he was at least a Protestant and Newcastle's loyalties seemed to now lie firmly with the Anglican Church. The initial coup was almost bloodless but troubles quickly flared in both Ireland and Scotland. It was not until 1715 that the contagion of rebellion sparked in the north-east.

In that year James III – the 'Old Pretender' – raised (or rather, had raised on his behalf) the standard of rebellion in Scotland. Here, the mercurial Earl of Mar, 'Bobbing John', drew out a largely highland army and fixed the White Cockade. In Northumberland recusant gentry, led (albeit reluctantly) by the Radcliffe Earl of Derwentwater, followed suit. These hard-riding gentry found little support for their prince's cause. Tradition relates that when they attempted to seize control of Newcastle, the citizens bellowed loud for King George – 'Geordie' – thus the enduring sobriquet. This may be apocryphal but these Northumbrian gentry remained very much isolated; finally galloping west towards Lancashire, Preston and bloody extinction.

Newcastle featured again in the Jacobite Rebellion of 1745 when ageing General Wade had forces stationed to resist another attempt, led this time by Prince Charles Edward, fantasist and dipsomaniac, otherwise known, to those who never met him, as 'Bonnie Prince

Charlie'. The Clans, ably led by Lord George Murray, wrong-footed the ponderous Wade and struck west at Carlisle. Lumbering after, the redcoats were mired in the filthy roads and barely crossed as far as Hexham. Thwarted, Wade fell back upon his considerable skills as an engineer to build perhaps his most famous highway – the Military Road from Newcastle to the Solway.

KING COAL

Six hundred years of sweat and toil
In that deep and dark abyss
The entrepreneur has spoken
Blown a tasteless goodbye kiss.
'The Last Northumbrian Coal Mine'
by John Robison

And then there was coal. During the medieval period all coal was referred to as 'sea' coal. This may have been because the coal was delivered out of the Tyne to London by ship, or because erosion of the exposed coal outcrops along the Tyne and Northumberland coast produced frequent quantities on beaches. The Northumbrian coastal measures appeared along the coast unlike in Durham where the seams were much deeper, thus the Durham measures were opened up much later.

In the thirteenth century Newcastle was considered primarily a source for leather hides and manufactured goods but the trade was damaged by the long years of the border wars and the reduction of the ready supplies of hides from Northumbrian beasts. However, coal was being mined at Whickham and Winlaton by the mid- to late thirteenth century and mines were soon being dug at Elswick, Heworth and on the Town Moor. By the mid-fifteenth century, 'keelmen' were already becoming an established monopoly. Following the Dissolution of the Established Church by Henry VIII and the rise of a new urban middle class, the mines flourished.

By 1787, over 7,000 miners worked in and around Newcastle. Early mines were shallow drifts or bell pits and many accidents occurred – men died at Whickham and Thrislington, for instance, as early as 1329. Causes of accidents tended to be collapse, explosion of gas and flooding. The miners were lowered up and down in buckets and if the shafts spread too far outwards, the weight of the roof and gear might produce a collapse. By the late sixteenth century mines were being sunk far deeper and horse-drawn engines, 'gin-gans', were employed to pump out excess water. Newcomen's 'fire' engines were being built after 1715 and Watt perfected his steam engine in 1769. Mechanical means could be harnessed to raise the coal and in 1753 Michael Menzies of Chartershaugh Colliery near Washington developed his own version – the 'Menzie'.

As mines became ever deeper, concerns over safety multiplied. As early as 1662 a petition signed by over 2,000 subscribers was submitted to parliament petitioning for improved means of ventilation; gas was always a killer and in the eighteenth century more and deadlier accidents occurred.

WORKSHOP OF THE WORLD

There was a time, through the nineteenth century, when Newcastle was the powerhouse of the world, a vast, sprawling industrial giant, inhabited by a race of titans; Stephensons, father and son, Swan, Hunter and Armstrong – several generations of engineering and entrepreneurial talent that changed Tyneside, Britain and the world. Dobson and Grainger created a cityscape to match this dynamic outpouring of innovation and the population multiplied exponentially – the outline of that old medieval centre subsumed if it was not fully erased. Railways sprang up over the city and county like a monstrous web, the railway and Central station altered the whole visual amenity, slashing relentlessly across contours of time in a breathless race for modernity. The Great Reform Act of 1832 (of which more later) had begun a process of enfranchisement allowing a newer mercantile class to intrude.

Steam was the driver, quite literally, of change. By 1814 the first steam-powered ferry, *Tyne Steam Packet* (later renamed as *Perseverance*), was sailing between Newcastle and Shields. The use of steam tugs which followed soon after ended a centuries-long tradition of closing the collieries for two of the winter months. Iron was now beginning to replace timber in ships and *Prince Albert*, the first to be built on

Tyneside, slid into the water in 1842. As industry began to boom, so mining began to decline, at least in the local context. Some new pits were opened but the High Main seam was becoming exhausted. From the 1820s new seams were being opened in County Durham and mining investment began to shift towards the east of that county.

Armstrong's great gun-works at Elswick spread over a wide acreage, giving employment to tens of thousands and became, with Krupps of Germany, the world's leading arms manufacturer. In an age of empire and with wars lighting up the globe, opportunity was never lacking. Armstrong's breech-loading field gun had revolutionised the face of battle, heralding the dawn of a new age of warfare. The ships built on Tyneside for the Imperial Japanese Navy, mounted with Armstrong's guns, smashed the Russians at Tsushima in 1905, the 'Trafalgar of the East'. The day of the Dreadnought, great armoured leviathans that rendered all previous classes of battle-cruiser utterly obsolete, had arrived. Prior to 1914 Britain and Germany embarked upon a Naval

Arms Race that would culminate in the blazing fury of Jutland during the First World War.

WORLD WARS

Both rural Northumberland and industrial Tyneside had been fertile recruiting ground for the armed forces in the First World War. That long martial tradition of border wars and bouts of economic recession ensured there were always more than a few who would take the king's shilling. When Kitchener pointed his famous finger, Geordies joined that ecstatic, doomed rush to the colours; thousands poured out their lifeblood, many thousands more came home maimed in mind and body. Unknown settlements in Belgium and France, unheard and unthought of, became household words of sorrow and loss.

'A land fit for heroes' proved to be something rather less, quite the reverse in fact. There was no glorious reawakening but only decline and despair. The great era of industrial dominance was ending, and its slow twilight was a time of hardship. Redundant workers marched on London in the famous Jarrow Hunger Marches as the gap between north and south yawned wider than ever before. Many lived in cramped, unsanitary housing where tuberculosis and other killer diseases stalked the slums with the relentlessness of a grim reaper. The 1930s, following the crash of 1929, were desperate times and depression bit deep.

In Europe the storm clouds were again gathering, especially after 1933 when Hitler came to power in Germany. Many young idealists from the left went off to Spain to fight in the chaotic Civil War there (1936–9). They served in the International Brigades fighting bloodily for the doomed, fissiparous Republicans, hamstrung equally by the indifference of the European democracies and their own fratricidal purges. Many did not return – those who did had achieved little more than a grim foretaste of what was to come. By a bizarre, historical irony the very evil of fascism was to produce an unexpected benefit to Tyneside with mass Jewish emigration from Germany.

KINDERTRANSPORT

There had been an established Jewish community in Newcastle during the early medieval period based around Silver Street (formerly Jew Gate). This community was re-established probably in the late eighteenth century, in about 1775, although no official record exists prior to 1830. During the nineteenth century the Jewish congregation was probably under 1,000. During the twentieth century the community expanded with several new synagogues, e.g. Gosforth opening in the suburbs. In the mid-nineteenth century an ultra orthodox group, led by Eliezer Adler and Zachariah Bernstone, fearing their Newcastle-based contemporaries were becoming over-lax, departed and crossed the river to locate themselves in Gateshead. The community quickly established itself as a major educational centre of Haredi (ultra conservative) Orthodox Jews; Talmudic students from across the globe came and continue to come to study at the religious institutions in the area.

The beginnings of the Nazi persecution after 1933 led to a very considerable spurt of immigration which considerably enlarged the community. Many of these were young people, children who formed part of the phenomenon known as the *Kindertransport* whereby thousands of Jewish children were moved out of Germany before the war, most if not all of whom would have been subsequently murdered had they been forced to remain. Most lost their families in the Holocaust. Nonetheless this wave of new blood into the region had a marked advantageous effect upon the local economy, then in the grip of the Depression. Adult émigrés who had been able to bring plant (rather than cash) resources used them to establish businesses in the area with many of them coming together to create what we know as the Team Valley Trading Estate.

Significant numbers of the immigrants had practical skills and experience which could be used to further the growth of those businesses while the high levels of education among them led many into professional careers. High percentages would become involved in medicine. Like so many migrants before and since, the very qualities which lead people to seek a new and better life elsewhere fitted them to achieve high levels of success in their new domicile. Hitler's vendetta provided an unintended benefit to Tyneside.

INTO THE FRONT-LINE: DAD'S ARMY

When the sirens first sounded in September 1939 and the lowering war clouds burst into downpour, there was no great rush to enlist, no great patriotic fervour, just grim resignation. After the disaster of Dunkirk as air raids over Tyneside increased, Anthony Eden had broadcast a call for volunteers to form what would become the Home Guard, immortalised as 'Dad's Army'. If one tours the north-east coast and inland, evidence of their activities abounds: Northumbrian beaches are studded with tank traps, concrete and steel gun emplacements, pillboxes and a superbly restored battery at Blyth.

In quiet Northumbrian lanes and in some most unexpected places one comes across further emplacements, seemingly in the most random pattern. These are, in fact, traces of the various 'stop' lines set up as a defence in depth against invasion. It was anticipated the Home Guard would be charged with resisting the initial onslaught on the beaches then holding a series of fallback positions to blunt the overall attack until a successful counter-attack could be launched. Most would have died or been captured.

From knobkerries and pikes to shotguns and rook rifles, the volunteers arrived armed with an antique arsenal of weapons, none suitable for fighting the Wehrmacht. One early suggestion was a form of pike constructed from a length of pipe fitted with a long, sword bayonet, effective if the enemy was obliging or chivalrous enough to permit the volunteer to get within stabbing range. Gradually a supply of rifles was sourced, some old US P17s from 1917, a reliable weapon although the round was incompatible with that of the Lee Enfield. Some of the US .45 cal. Thompson or 'Tommy' guns were provided, the sort of gun most Englishmen had only witnessed in the hands of James Cagney or George Raft.

DAD'S ARMY SPECIAL FORCES – THE AUXILIARIES

For those members of the Home Guard who showed a special aptitude there was a secret guerrilla army; highly trained to cause maximum disruption to any invading Germans. Little is known about these

Auxiliary Units, even today, but there were three battalions covering Scotland, northern England and southern England and full of the cream of the Home Guard. These men, all hand-picked volunteers, laid down months of supplies of both arms and food, ready to go into hiding the day the invasion started. Their job was to slow the invasion down by blowing up arms and fuel dumps, bridges, railway lines and generally causing confusion to the invaders. Life expectancy was considered around 14 days.

POST-INDUSTRIAL TYNESIDE

We'll not forget you Thatcher
And your heartless decimation
Your ultimate achievement
A bitter divided nation.
'The Last Northumbrian Coal Mine'
by John Robinson

For Britain as a whole and noticeably on Tyneside, the post-war period was one characterised initially by austerity and then by a cycle of 'boom and bust'. More will be said in the following chapters on politics, industry, cultural and social trends but, between 1945 and the Millennium, Newcastle changed faster and more profoundly than at any other time in its long history. Old industries finally faded away, the mines declined, were nationalised then spluttered on into the bitterness of the 1984 Miners' Strike. Shipbuilding, heavy engineering and armaments dwindled and largely if not completely disappeared. At the same time employment in the public and services sector increased dramatically, Newcastle became retail heaven, a legend in its own hedonistic night-time; student city and party town, home of *Viz* and the Fat Slags.

Social mobility came of age in the era of the Welfare State and 'you've never had it so good.' The suburban and garden city boom of pre-war southern England finally came north, vast swathes of new uniform, 'executive' dwellings, link villas and latterly trendy Quayside apartments, blossomed in a seemingly endless process of gobbling up green pastures and brownfield sites alike. Car ownership rocketed from one per street to two per family, fast trains could get you to

London in three hours, the plane in less than one. Package holidays and second homes abroad moved from the exotic to commonplace. Footballers were paid staggering sums while whole areas fell into decline. The Meadow-Well Estate in North Tyneside festered then flared in the 1990s.

That great public sector dream of universal housing, of towering tower blocks, built largely on nepotism and corruption turned sour, its messiah turned bad, was brought low and discredited. The legacy, ironically lives on, the blocks still tower as it would cost too much to pull them down and there's no replacement housing available. They decay as the bitter inheritance of jerry building matures; grim warrens where no hope or aspiration can flourish. But the story continues.

3

ANATOMY OF A CITY – AN URBAN LANDSCAPE

MEDIEVAL TOWNSCAPE

Newcastle was, by the time of the Civil War, among the four largest towns in the country and one of the wealthiest. A map of 1638 showing the defences also gives us invaluable information on the layout and density of the wards. These extended beyond the walls to the north at New Gate and Pilgrim Street Gate, to the west at West Gate and, most of all, in the east at Sandgate. Not all was boom and prosperity; around 41 per cent of households were defined as being 'in poverty' in 1665.

It is certain that the more affluent wards clustered in the centre, (Castle, Guildhall and Quayside), while poorer wards pressed against the town's ancient walls in the north-east and north-west with the exception of Sandgate which, while on the outskirts, hugged the course of the river. The medieval guild structure had, in previous centuries, led to 'occupational zoning and social class mixing'. Guild members tended to live close to each other; workshop and/ or warehouse occupied the same plot as living quarters for master and family with journeymen apprentices and servants living in the upper quarters of the same building. By the mid-seventeenth century this historic pattern was breaking down as wealthier members of the community, particularly the merchant elite, were developing links with the gentry of the surrounding countryside and buying properties outside the city, thus beginning a process of 'gentrification' by progressive disassociation with the urban sprawl – a trend which continued into the twentieth century.

By the seventeenth century, with the Scottish threat apparently removed, those great traders of the town had become bankers to the whole region, from Tees to Tweed. Money flowed out to lord and landlords from the north. Newcastle provided much-needed liquid cash to replace it. Certain, select hostmen acted as bankers on an even greater scale. In 1623, Sir William Selby, part of a group of northern merchants which included the Delavals and the Belaysyses, was recorded as lending money to London. Merchants formed a cash-rich monopoly based on swelling profits from the burgeoning coal trade. Banking status ensured Newcastle's hostmen were creditors to both landlord and tenant, 'This towne unto this countrye, serves in stead of London: by means whereof the countrye is supplied with money.'

The banking role of Newcastle's merchants was almost unique and gave them significant control over debtors as well as an opportunity to generate significant returns for themselves. It also meant that these financiers were in a position to enter into joint ventures with gentry anxious to put their lands to commercial use; relationships that might well be cemented in other ways, ideally by dynastic marriages.

DRIVERS OF PROSPERITY

'King Coal' was not the only significant generator of economic prosperity – the cloth trade, maritime activity, leather working, glass and salt-making (there were salt pans at South Shields and some at North Shields) all played their part. In terms of cultural life, which clings to the coat tails of economic prosperity, the town was exhibiting levels of sophistication. Chamberlains' accounts record payments to travelling players, poets and entertainers and the urban centre acted as a cultural as well as commercial magnet – many of the Northumbrian gentry had town houses, providing opportunities to boost affinities.

Following the Dissolution and 'privatisation' of the mines fuelling an upsurge in mining activity during the 1580s, the city was able to respond to the diminishing importance of previously crucial economic activity such as the production and processing of wool. Newcastle was in an ideal position to supply cheap fuel; deposits were close to the surface, extracted from easily accessed pits. Coal could then be transported by water to the city for shipping on to London.

The 'Grand Lease' (meaning the rights to exploit mines in Whickham and Gateshead) had been assigned by Queen Elizabeth to a consortium of Newcastle-based merchants. By the turn of the seventeenth century, the city was exporting 150,000 tons per year rising to 300,000 tons to London alone in 1650.

The trade became an increasingly significant occupation for those deprived of other employment outside the city. The turbulent border which had provided employment of a sort, usually violent and illicit, had ceased to exist as an economic factor in that sense. Between 1565 and 1625 the coal trade increased twelve fold. Newcastle coal owners opined that 5,800 men were employed in the Tyneside coal industry in 1637–8. Those other local industries mentioned above – cloth, maritime activity, leather working, glass and salt-making – were increasingly dependant on coal as a ready source of fuel.

MEDIEVAL WALLS

In 1644 the ancient walls still stood some 12ft in height, with a thickness of 8ft and fronted by a ditch or fosse some 22 yards wide and 8ft in depth. Gates were 'embattled' and the enceinte studded with strong towers 'between each of which, there were for the most part two watch towers made square with effigies of men cut in stone upon the top of them as though they were watching, and they are called garret, which had square holes over the walls to through [throw] stones down. '

All of the towers were constructed with a rounded outer face and rectangular inner elevation. This was a form designed to frustrate or limit the effectiveness of mining, very much a medieval tactic which was to feature extensively in the siege of 1644. In the south-west corner the circuit commenced with the Riverside Tower which stood to the left (looking from inside-out) of the Close Gate. From here, on the level riverside, the line ran sharply uphill broken by the Whitefriar

Tower, which derived its name from the adjoining Carmelite Friary (a postern had been knocked through for the convenience of the friars). Here, the Masons Guild met in the upper storey while the bricklayers used the lower level. Northwards, next came Neville Tower and the family's town residence, Westmorland House, stood nearby. Next the circuit looped off north-west to reach the formidable West Gate which the Elizabethan antiquary Leland described as 'a mightye strong thing'. It was frequently employed as a gaol.

None of the quartet of towers along this section has survived. That which ran parallel to Stowell Street, past St Andrews to the New Gate has fared rather better though frustratingly, the portal itself has gone. Herber Tower, described by Bourne as 'not only the strongest but also the most antient [ancient] of all the other gates', was the meeting house of the felt makers, curriers and armourers, while Morden Tower accommodated glaziers, pewterers, and painters. From New Gate the line continued in an easterly direction along the line of Blackett Street to Pilgrim Gate then to Carliol Tower. Here the wall bends south down to the well-preserved, though altered Plummer Tower (Cutler's Guild), past Austin Tower, a corner turret, then Pandon Gate; Wall Knoll Tower (Carpenters); the Sally Port (so called as this was a postern enabling the garrison to mount a raid or sally) and across City Road to Sand Gate. This was so called as it was built upon the alluvial sands; it was demolished in the eighteenth century as a safety hazard.

THE PRE-CLASSICAL ERA

In 1644 these noble walls would resume their former significance and become the very symbol of the townspeople's resistance, a fusion of status and function dictated by expediency and dire need! Those of the better sort, the merchant-princes, still had their town houses in the old mercantile heart – the Close and Sandhill where stood tall and stately timber-framed houses, lit by casemented windows. Waterways such as the Lort Burn which Speed's map of 1610 shows as running north to south through the centre, steep-sided and choked with noxious refuse, were as yet left uncovered. In the Side were many shops and artisans dwellings. Sandhill remained the municipal heart of the city, where coal barons and shippers conducted business and held court. Less prosaically, Sandhill also housed the fish-market.

To the north the Bigg Market, Oat and Flesh Markets teemed – these last two were divided by a double row of residential properties with the aptly named Middle Street running centrally between. The Flesh Market was, in part, given over to the sale of cloth – the Cloth-Market which hosted two annual fairs granted by medieval charter. Standing northwards beyond Bigg Market was a residential street, Hucksters' Booths in Newgate Street. East of this lay Pilgrim Street regarded then as being the most agreeable thoroughfare in the city; those of the lesser sort lived beyond the centre in diminishing splendour.

So the heart of the medieval plan remained as the jewel with some grand residences such as Anderson Place, built in the wake of the Dissolution on the site of the former Grey Friars beyond. The streets would resonate with noise, narrow, cramped, verminous and reeking. The sixteenth and seventeenth centuries were a period when those of

Bessie Surtees' House, typical of the timber-framed townhouses of the sixteenth and seventeenth century, a glimpse of the historic quayside.

wealth still lived in the centre, though many now did have country houses, the process of suburbanisation had not truly begun and the diaspora from the core lay in the future.

BUILDERS AND BUILDINGS

Sir Niklaus Pevsner believed Newcastle to be the best designed Victorian town in England. The city has more listed Georgian buildings than anywhere else in the country outside London and Bath, and Grey Street has been voted the best street in Britain on a number of occasions.

What is the link between Newcastle and Australia? Building of course; the Tyne Bridge was based on the design of the great Sydney Harbour Bridge. We returned the favour though. Multi-disciplinary consulting engineers Ove Arup (who were responsible for Central Square, Newcastle) completed the structural design of Sydney Opera House. Central Square is an outstanding example of modern architecture: a 1930s post office sorting station converted into office space reminiscent of art deco New York. The central atrium is covered in the same material as the Millennium Dome and is self-cleaning. Central Square North and South are surrounded by modern art, including a striking two-storey sculpture of a forearm. This was first wrapped in black plastic when it was lowered into place one quiet Sunday morning in 2002, looking for all the world as though it was wearing a rubber glove ready for celestial washing up!

Tyneside flats were responsible for making our area one of the most overcrowded in England. These two-storey terraces, with flats on each floor, have separate front doors and rear staircases. They date from the 1840s and had become so much a part of the Newcastle scene by the end of the century that legislation was introduced controlling their dimensions. The terraces must be at least 40ft apart at the front, 20ft at the rear and rooms have to be at least 70 sq ft.

CITY OF DOBSON & GRAINGER

If he was alive today Richard Grainger, born in 1797, would probably be sneered at as an 'entrepreneur' or more pithily, a 'spiv'. The early twenty-first century is an age of sneering and of puritanical disdain for those who glorify material success and a hearty condemnation of those who achieve it. Grainger would probably drive a Range Rover or BMW 4WD with personalised number plate and reside in Darras Hall. Nonetheless, in the thrusting, Whiggish climate of two centuries ago, his achievement and lasting impact were very considerable.

He began as a property developer in 1819 or 1820 when he erected his initial domestic, terrace scheme in Higham Place, followed by a rash of similar projects. Eight years later, using his wife's substantial dowry of £5,000, he undertook an initial commercial venture on Blackett Street. During the late 1820s and 1830s his output was prolific, working with architects such as John Dobson and Thomas Oliver. He built Eldon Square (1825–9) and Leazes Terrace (1829–34). The Royal Arcade on Pilgrim Street which dates from 1831 to 1832 was firstly intended as a new corn exchange but political support, at this juncture, was lacking and he was obliged to gamble on retail in the hope the new railway station would be built nearby; as mentioned above, this scheme ultimately failed. This would not be the last time Grainger got it wrong where the railway was concerned,

Grainger acquired a further, ardent collaborator in the shape of local lawyer John Clayton, a remarkable character himself. Clayton was town clerk (akin to a 'CEO'), a highly influential appointment, and the town council, at this time, was anxious to support new and prestigious development. Grainger's stylish and grandiose schemes fitted perfectly with the rise of the great industrial centre and thrusting middle classes. His earlier solicitor, John Fenwick, had suggested the developer move his legal affairs to Clayton's firm. Not only was Clayton town clerk and legal advisor to the developer but also an investor, a speculator in modern terms, in these developments. At the time this was entirely overt and no likely conflicts were perceived. These new men – Dobson, Grainger and Clayton, a formidable triumvirate – were a nineteenth-century elite, the new commercial and corporate entity; their oligarchic predecessors would have understood perfectly.

A NEW HEART FOR THE TOWN

Grainger's masterpiece was breathtaking in vision and boldness, redrawing the map of Newcastle to shift the axis of prosperity away from the traditional riverfront towards the upper town. The Lort Burn would be filled in and the higher section of Dean Street constructed running from Mosley Street up towards Blackett Street. Grainger Street would be built to stretch from the junction of these new boulevards towards the Bigg Market. Clayton Street would stretch further west to Newgate Street and Westgate. The old Theatre Royal in Mosley Street and the meat market (only completed barely two decades before) were casualties and both had to be rebuilt as part of the scheme – civic gain in modern parlance.

The concept moved with audacious speed. Vast quantities of earth were transported to dump into the Lort Burn and, almost within a year, the new Grainger Market with its 180 shops was opened and trading; within four years the rest was built. Some 2,000 navvies and artisans were employed throughout, nine new civic streets of astonishing elegance and proportion transformed the cityscape; 10 inns, 12 pubs, 325 shops with accommodation and 40 gentlemen's residences completed it. The superb new Theatre Royal and Central Exchange added cultural pearls to the commercial lustre. Some years later, one correspondent wrote of the Newspaper Room in the new Exchange 'it is, in the leisure hours of the evening, in the Central Exchange, that the mind relaxes and is relieved from the fag of business, from the tension and anxiety of commercial enterprise.'

THE FINEST OF CITYSCAPES

In 1836, Upper Dean Street was renamed as Grey Street to commemorate Lord Grey and his role in the passing of the Great Reform Act in 1832. Two years later, the political titan's towering and elegant memorial was thrown up at the very hub of the new centre where it remains, both monument and beacon. There was no cost-cutting; the entire project came in at a very hefty £646,000, a staggering sum at the time. Faced in ashlar, with bespoke drainage and supply, lit by gas, streets macadamised, the Dobson/Grainger/Clayton collaboration produced one of the country's finest provincial centres. The wonderfully elegant curve of Grey Street as it dips towards Dean Street with the sterling spire of Grey's Monument is the view which defines Newcastle.

In an influential essay, historian Thomas Faulkner likens the heady atmosphere of this period to the service sector boom of strident Thatcherism and watered down version under Blair. There is clearly some truth in this, though one feels bound to observe that the elegance and durability of Grainger's vision is likely to outlast that of his more contemporary successors – indeed, modern utilitarian building in Newcastle reeks mostly of dour expediency.

VICTORIAN SUBURBS

Grainger's schemes redrew the urban map, yet the drive for such ventures and the cash to fund them came from burgeoning industry. Grainger sought to capitalise further, adding to his already massive debt by acquiring the Elswick Estate to the west of the town centre, gambling this would secure the site for any future central station. Again he miscalculated and, barely a year after his great scheme for the centre was completed, he was facing ruin. The canny Clayton steered him clear of bankruptcy, although at the date of his death in 1861, Grainger still owed £128,582. Dobson followed four years later leaving a respectable if relatively modest estate of £16,000. Clayton, the lawyer who lived until ripe old age, dying in 1890, left a substantial £729,000.

METROPOLIS

Grainger fed civic pride but this did not relieve the pressure created by a swelling population. Newcastle's magnetism, as industry flourished and boomed after 1850, caused immigration to soar. Population rocketed from 88,000 in 1851, to 128,000 twenty years later; 186,000 by 1891 and to 267,000 by 1911. In part this demand

was satisfied by throwing up mass housing specifically intended to service giant concerns such as Armstrong's gun works and the shipyards; acre after acre of uniform terrace housing, red brick, solid, if often crowded and damp. As mentioned above, the unique 'Tyneside Flat' was part of this response. Apartment type living was a Tyneside phenomenon – by 1911, 44.5 per cent of the city's inhabitants dwelled in flats, against a national average of only 3.7 per cent. In areas, formerly villages, such as Elswick where Armstrong's industry provided the driver, population swelled from 400 in 1811 to 14,345 mid-century.

Elswick was by no means the only such suburban community to sprout. Along the river, at Walker, Byker and Benwell, street upon street of terraced housing arose, the familiar 'back-to-backs' that were to remain a feature of the extended urban sprawl until the improver's scythe began to cut them down en masse in the 1960s and '70s. This crowding density, springing up on the river banks, was paralleled by a more genteel process on the more northerly, landward flank.

The imposing breadth of the Town Moor, nearly 1,000 acres, remained as a bulwark against unchecked expansion but east of the open expanse Jesmond blossomed into a model enclave. Armstrong's hand could be detected here also as, from 1883, the Dene, a tumbling romantic fantasy, was gifted by him to the city. Here streets were broad and elegant, pleasing terraces and imposing dwellings of the higher bourgeoisie. As Pevsner observed, 'there are none of the Gothic door-cases, shafted windows and turreted roofs then fashionable elsewhere in England; just good bricks and slates and good craftsmanship with perhaps, some bands of coloured brick, pierced bargeboards and castellated chimney pots.'

THE EARLY TWENTIETH CENTURY

Despite the deep recession after 1918 the city continued to expand and estates such as Pendower, Longbenton and the Ridges (Meadow Well), were constructed between the wars on the garden suburb model. Pre-war developers, particularly William Leech, began to provide affordable, low-cost housing for those aspiring to home ownership, bringing artisan and council worker into the status of proprietorship. The era is viewed as being characterised by depression and decline, squalor and means testing. Both had marked and pernicious effects but, at the same time, there was a rising level of confidence in certain sectors, a Leech House cost around £400–£500 and a tradesman might earn £3 a week. This was not the boom seen further south but a strong and resounding echo.

Another dynamic at work, before and after the Second World War, most markedly after, was the shifting balance between road and rail. The great era of steam which had seen the city much altered by the thrusting confidence of railway lines was now being usurped by motor transport. From the 1930s, cheaper, mass-produced cars began to place motor travel within the reach of the average family, stirrings of a revolution that would flower in the 1960s.

One of the marvels of Tyneside, and perhaps its most recognisable icon, is the Tyne Bridge, constructed during the 1920s. A smaller

The Tyne Bridge at sunset, perhaps for many the defining image of Newcastle.

version of its internationally renowned cousin in Sydney, it has come to define our predominant image of city and river.

CITY IN THE SKY

The ten towers of the flats are a familiar part of the Newcastle skyline and have turned up in a number of TV shows from *Whatever Happened to the Likely Lads?* to *55 Degrees North*. They were thrown up in the 1960s as part of T. Dan Smith's flawed vision of a 'city in the sky'. Like so many buildings of that era they have needed serious attention over the years partly because of the design but also in an attempt to revitalise a neighbourhood which was notable for high levels of deprivation and crime. The latest attempt was announced in 2010; five of the blocks are to be demolished, the remainder revamped (with some to be sold off for owner occupation) and the area is to be renamed which will help, of course.

The design, like so many of this period in Newcastle, was based on a Swedish model. The name Cruddas Park is taken from George Cruddas, a director of the nearby Armstrong's factory where so many people in the small terraced rows the flat replaced were once employed. His former home, Dene House, was demolished to make way for one of the blocks, though one suspects it was built to a somewhat higher standard.

Back in the 1980s a labour mayor of the city lived in one of the upper levels. Newcastle mayors are entitled to display symbols of office outside their residences, including a Victorian-style lamp post. I wish I had been there the day they installed that on the outside of a 23-storey building!

Not that these are the tallest buildings in the city. That honour goes to Vale House in Sandyford. Built in 1968, it is 80 metres tall and has 28 floors. Largely residential, utterly depressing, it has 138 flats.

Newcastle would become the Brasilia of the north, a dark and sterile Camelot of the masses. Re-routing would see traffic relegated to ground level while the population lived in the light and air above, negotiating the town via a series of walkways. Some of these can still be seen, crossing the motorway from the city centre to the east end. Massive and monumental buildings of accursed Swedish design (like the Civic Centre and unspeakable Swan House) would assert the place of Newcastle in the twentieth century. Modernity was king. Much of the older part of the city was demolished to make way for new shopping areas and high rises, many of them regarded as monstrous eyesores in subsequent decades. For years, one of them, Westgate House, would top local polls for detested buildings. It even made it into a list of the dozen most hated buildings in the country when Channel Four conducted a national poll in 2005.

This is ironic because the street which always makes it into the most desirable list, nationally and internationally, is Grey Street with its long sweep of classical buildings; it continues to do so, the latest accolade being the Academy of Urbanism's 'Great Street' Award in 2010.

THE BRASILIA OF THE NORTH

Old Scotswood Road must live again
To carry further still its fame.
We're soon to have a celebration –
Let Tyneside rise in jubilation.

From Cruddas Park to Rye Hill
We are determined, have the will
That horrid slums we shall erase
With surgeon's knife and then replace.

This unfortunate doggerel was the work of Thomas Daniel Smith, a better politician than poet who, before his fall, stood as a titan of the left, of the new and progressive whose ethos had a significant impact during the heady boom years of the 1960s. Of impeccable working class credentials, T. Dan Smith was born in 1915 and trained and worked as painter and decorator; despite radical political beliefs he built up a chain of businesses, not necessarily on the back of quality workmanship, avoided service in the Second World War as a conscientious objector, entering local politics in 1952. As a socialist he more resembled the parochial French version, an artisan of expressed views with a firm belief in self-determination rather than rigid orthodoxy, one who saw no conflict between radical philosophy and *petite bourgeoisie* capitalist enterprise. His rise in the party was meteoric and influential; his vision of Newcastle as sweeping as that of Grainger a century beforehand.

BUILD FAST, BUILD CHEAP, BUILD UPWARDS!

By the mid-1960s as Labour, under Harold Wilson, finally toppled the long Conservative ascendancy, Smith dominated the local political skyline. Like Grainger he understood the value and practice of showmanship, socialism through good PR. And it worked. Smith's dynamic new vision was so in keeping with the iconoclastic spirit of the decade, new motorways would set a grid pattern, the Quayside; long since sunk into terminal disrepair, was to be revitalised. Eldon Square would be reborn and a central 'Cultural Plaza' created around the new Central Library. Thomas Faulkner records that, 'Smith and his Associates . . . were seeking what they saw as a clean, new, international image which they believed would dispel unfavourable industrial myths and attract new businesses.'

History has taken a pejorative view of Smith. His career was to sink ingloriously in a mire of corruption barely a decade later – and of his vision which, unlike that of Grainger, was not based upon a Whiggish philosophy of prosperity through progress and reward on investment, but upon a utopian vision, funded from taxpayers, radical and, to a degree, totalitarian. Grainger invested in quality, Smith did not; he built fast, upwards and on the cheap. Again in line with the Gallic model of socialist endeavour, he was happy to profit from this vast expenditure by awarding lucrative contracts to his own web of companies. It was his relationship with Pontefract-based architect John Poulson, described as one who knew everyone had a price and possessed the knack of assessing the requisite scale of bribery accordingly, which brought him down.

ELDON SQUARE AND THE LATER TWENTIETH CENTURY

T. Dan Smith and his immediate successors were no respecters of history. From the ideological viewpoint of the 1960s, the 'old' simply implied slums, degradation and squalor. Much of what was swept away needed demolition but what replaced it, most noticeably in the case of concrete and steel leviathans stretching towards the distant skies, very quickly degenerated into something not a great deal better. The new central shopping arcade of Eldon Square vandalised much of Dobson and Grainger's elegant vision in the 1970s and the Central Motorway East hacked through the cityscape in a manner Pevsner aptly describes as 'brutally assertive'. It was indeed a period both of brutality and assertiveness. The New Central Library, one of the showpieces of our northern Brasilia and constructed between 1966 and 1968, was only recently replaced. The Cultural Plaza around very quickly went to seed in which unhappy state it has remained.

Back-to-back housing in Byker was superseded by Ralph Erskine's grandiose Wall, a monumental construction which as now gravitated to iconic status. Pevsner approves, '[it] shows how a community and designers could work together to rebuild a neighbourhood in a comfortable and practical way.' Many, including the present writer, would disagree.

A singularly disastrous experiment was the extension of Killingworth in the late 1960s, designed by Roy Gazzard on the lines of a medieval township and culminating in a 'citadel' of monumental ugliness. More Stalinist than Gothic, the concept, once executed, quickly turned sour, dirty and decayed. The crippling weakness of much post-war development was not just the unsound, ideologically driven process but the extremely shoddy mode of building. Both have left a bad legacy. Tower blocks became damp and unsightly slums with maintenance costs spiralling, people within trapped and isolated in an Orwellian nightmare.

NEWCASTLE CIVIC CENTRE

Which building in the city took nearly thirty years to finish? Newcastle first drew up plans for a new civic centre at Barras Bridge in 1939 when a competition was held to find the winning design. War and shortages held matters up and it was not until 1956 that the project got underway. Work on the site did not in fact begin until 1960. It cost a total of £4,855,000 and was only finished in 1968. The great, grandiose chandelier in the formal entrance comprises eleven tiers, topped with four seahorses, one of Newcastle's civic symbols.

THE WREN STONE

What is Newcastle's connection to that great baroque architect Sir Christopher Wren? At the foot of the tower in the north-west corner of the Civic Centre lies the Wren Stone, a gift to the city. The stone was personally selected at the quarries by Sir Christopher Wren for the building of St Paul's Cathedral and bears his insignia of approval.

At the north end of Ceremonial Way, mounted on a Norwegian Otta slate flank wall forming the link to the Council Chamber, is a bronze sculpture of the River God Tyne by David Wynne. It measures 16ft high and weighs in at 2¼ tons). When it was first erected it became the single largest bronze figure to be erected in this country in the twentieth century.

The River God was taken off his platform (metaphorically) when Newcastle and Gateshead attempted to win 'European City of Culture 2008'. He was turned into a cartoon figure in a promotional film, flying over the city and citing our many virtues. Sadly a lot of these revolved round our reputation as party city and the judges decided in favour of Liverpool. Maybe he should have stayed out of the Bigg Market.

He did manage a few other landings. Carved in 1786, he graces one of the arches at Somerset House, London; one of nine carvings symbolising Britain's rivers. He is crowned with flaming coals which, together with pick and shovel, birds, fish and nets, represent Tyneside's early industries. He also had a place on the wall of the Tyne Rowing Club's boathouse near Newburn.

MILLENNIUM

Tyneside's Millennium Bridge, an elegantly curved engineering marvel, has added a further star to the pantheon of famous Tyne bridges. It is a very worthy addition, linking the twin cultural foci of Newcastle and Gateshead Quaysides. Few keelmen or even those alive during the Second World War and the immediate post-war era when this writer was born and growing up, would recognise Newcastle Quayside. Previously, there was decay and ruin, the tattered ghost of a once-famous port and shipbuilding hub. On Gateshead side the Sage and Baltic Mill have created a wholly new dynamic, culture and leisure superseding centuries of commerce and industry.

If the 1960s vision of dark utopia ended in a mire of greed and corruption, leaving a legacy of Stalinist decay, the 1980s brought back greed. Indeed, it was fashionable. In political terms the north-east rejected Thatcherism. This became the anathema of the prevailing left. The much-hyped and overstated myth of the 1984 Miners' Strike became a hallowed, propagandist icon. Beneath the veneer of disdain, however, there was a boom. The service sector, lawyers, accountants and financial services created a regional hub as Newcastle serves a large hinterland and this was a decade when anything was possible. The city was likened to its larger Yorkshire rival, Leeds. The SME sector, fuelled by a ready cash supply from a raft of hungry bankers, spawned a host of new enterprises. Sir John Hall, perhaps and certainly for many, the face of the new regional capitalism, created his grand temple complex of retail Babel at the Metrocentre.

Interior designers, bespoke retailers and trendy clothes boutiques flourished, great swathes of new housing crowded the once-green spaces of North Tyneside. Leech, Bellway and Barratt all competed to throw up mass housing schemes to meet a seemingly inexhaustible demand. On Newcastle's Quayside and further east at Walker, executive or 'yuppie' enclaves appeared, linked to marinas and offering lifestyle choice. A rash of new and self-important hotels – the Copthorne at Closegate being the first – broadcast the city's status as regional capital. The Northern Development Company, a dynamic force soon to be succeeded by the lacklustre and top heavy Regional Development Agency, was energetic in drawing in substantive manufacturing investment.

BOOM AND BUST

This hedonistic boom of the 1980s came crashing down in the early 1990s when the banks realised their lending books were wildly exposed and their clients, in many cases, impossibly geared. Much pain was inflicted yet, by the Millennium, most of the gloom had dissipated and a further cycle of boom was spawned, one that had apparently learned nothing from the last. Throughout the early years of the first decade of the twenty-first century, while the myth of Tony Blair's celestial omnipotence somehow, against all the evidence, persisted, and one disastrous foreign adventure followed another, the housing market surged as never before. Lenders crowded the market, anxious to lend in virtually every circumstance. Green-and brownfield schemes abounded, the old industries merely a largely forgotten facet of heritage.

Many of the older, 1960s type office blocks such as Carliol House and Cale Cross House proved embarrassingly difficult to let, and a rash of new office building crowded the regenerated Quayside reaching westwards. Rank folly on the part of the board of Northern Rock plc, previously the region's leading blue chip lender, began the toppling of dominos which ushered in the prevailing recession. Overnight building ceased, developers were left with hugely expensive, suddenly unsaleable schemes on their books and not a friendly bank manager in sight.

Much of what was new stayed virgin; builders inevitably became the first casualties and a pall of gloom spread over the once brightly lit horizon as austerity bit home. In spite of this spinning rollercoaster the late twentieth century witnessed a major physical transformation in the city – some was good, at its best very good and much was and remains bad. In the main, these newer commercial buildings are almost uniformly hideous. Government Office North East is situated in a monolithic slab of cut-price Stalinist chic at Citygate. Much of the new build in that area is equally depressing; nonetheless there are some fine examples where creative talent and quality of construction have been allowed to combine.

HOW MANY TIMES WILL HYDE PARK FIT INTO THE TOWN MOOR?

Two and a half times; the Moor is unique and it is the largest area of preserved common land close to a city centre in the whole of Britain. Although, technically, it is not really a common but a land grant, King John gave the original (smaller) moor to the town in 1213 (no wonder they called him 'Lackland'). The Freemen of the City retained the right to graze their livestock there and still do so today (which is why you see so many cows wandering around).

It was formally sold to the Town Council in 1885 for £2,200 and is today jointly run by Council and Freemen. Protected and regulated by statute (the most recent Town Moor Act was passed in 1988), the Act statutes restrict building on the open ground though there are some tenants. Best known of these is Newcastle United FC who rent St James' Park from the city. Part of the rent is passed on to the Freemen to use in maintaining the Moor.

THE RVI

Originally founded as the Newcastle Infirmary in 1751, the Royal Victoria Infirmary (RVI) was opened on 11 July 1906 by Edward VII, built on 10 acres of Town Moor given by the Corporation and Freemen. Like many hospitals it has been the beneficiary of a number of legacies over the years including, it is said, one from Queen Victoria who left some of her underwear to the institution. That's a sizeable gift – another set which went on sale in London recently had a 51in waist.

The hospital was built to mark the Jubilee of Queen Victoria in 1897. Organiser of the Diamond Jubilee Fund (which raised a staggering £110,000), was Sir Riley Lord (yes, we have got the name the right way round) who had made his fortune as chief representative of the Prudential, a major insurance company. He was a self-made man who had started work as a block printer at the age of eight. After work, he attended classes at Acrrington Mechanics' Institute to improve himself; truly a self-made man in the best Victorian mould. He was almost a northern Dick Whittington, except that he was thrice Lord Mayor of Newcastle rather than London.

The new hospital had a reputation to maintain. Even in the nineteenth century, hospitals were aware of the risks from medical mistakes.

On the administration of anaesthetic (1888):

> The administrator is to give his undivided attention to his important duty.

> The administrator, on every occasion, is to be provided with a tongue forceps, and a hypodermic syringe filled with ether, and is to see that a portable electrical battery is ready at hand.

WHERE WAS NEWCASTLE'S
VERSION OF HARLEY STREET?

Ellison Place in the city centre housed a surprising number of medical practitioners and supporters, and all from a philanthropic ship owner who made substantial donations to the Diamond Jubilee fund which built the RVI to a manufacturer of medical rubber. A number of doctors had homes here, including the Hume family. George Haliburton Hume had been honorary surgeon to the Newcastle Infirmary. His son, William Errington Hume, held the Chair of Medicine at the Newcastle Medical School.

The third medical generation was represented by Dr John Hume whose brother, initially named George Haliburton after their grandfather, is better known as Cardinal Basil Hume (he took Basil as his name in orders when he became a monk). Oddly enough, the father of this most significant Catholic was a Protestant who met his wife, Marie Elizabeth Tisseyre, while serving in France during the First World. As was normal in 'mixed marriages' at this time, the children were brought up in their mother's faith.

A statue commemorating the cardinal's life and achievement stands outside St Mary's Cathedral in a peaceful square just off Neville Street. He is shown wearing simple monk's robe and the cross of local saint, Cuthbert. His plinth is carved into the shape of Lindisfarne Holy Island, reflecting his affection for Northumberland and its spiritual history.

Ellison Place housed other professions. A medical galvanist practised there, administering electric shocks – popular nineteenth-century treatment for a range of illnesses. Lodgings for circuit judges were provided in a house at the junction and a company of pharmaceutical suppliers were just around the corner in Northumberland Road. The latter had a company logo which can still be seen on the front of their building (now a set of student flats). Brady & Martin inserted a couple of superscript (and very tiny) 'e's just above Brady's name so that it could be read as 'Be Ready'.

ACCIDENTS DO HAPPEN

Take a look at the churches in Northumberland Road, both of them delightful buildings. But you are actually looking at three churches. Holy Trinity (now used by Northumbria University) is a rebuild. Roman Catholics from the parish did not have resources to put up their own building so purchased a second-hand church from nonconformists. Stone by stone they moved it from its original location on New Bridge Street. However, somewhere along the way, something went missing – the original church had two turrets, this has only one.

4

CITIZENS OF NOTE
& NOTORIETY

AETHELFRITH (d. AD 616)

Known as 'the Destroyer', Aethelfrith was largely responsible for the
expansion of the Anglian kingdom in the late sixth and early seventh
centuries. Possibly an illegitimate grandson of Ida who founded the
Saxon enclave of Bernicia, Aethelfrith had links with the Pictish
kingdoms to the north and smashed the Scots of Dalriada at the
battle of Daegsastan (possibly Dissington near Ponteland) in about
603. Prior to that he'd met the northern Britons (the 'Goddodin') in
battle at Catreath (Catterick) and trounced them. After a shotgun
wedding with the daughter of the adjacent Anglian state of Deira
(Durham and Cleveland), he arranged for the death of his father-
in-law and drove his brother-in-law and future nemesis Edwin into
hunted exile.

This was but the beginning of a pattern of conquest that saw the
infant kingdom of Northumbria rise to prominence at the start
of what has been dubbed the 'Heroic' Age. Aethelfrith came to
dominate northern England and his expansion led to a quarrel
with Welsh princes and a great battle at Chester in 616. Here,
the pagan Northumbrians not only defeated their Christian foes
but slaughtered a contingent of monks to make their point more
fully. Their crowning triumph was short lived. King Raedwald of
East Anglia championed the cause of the exiled Edwin, by now
also Christian and the destroyer was in turn destroyed in a furious
Gotterdammerung by the River Idle, thus Edwin became king and
brought the Christian faith to Northumbria.

BEDE (AD 672/673–735)

The Venerable Bede was a monk of St Peter's at Wearmouth. This monastery, together with its twin foundation, St Paul's at Jarrow, had been constructed a generation beforehand by Benedict Biscop, the leading churchman of his day. Benedict was a great builder on a grand scale – his two churches were the first to be erected in stone with masons imported from the Continent. Both glowed with rich adornment and had become a potent symbol of what was now the 'Golden' Age of Northumbria. After the death of Oswiu's successor Ecgfrith in a disastrous encounter with a Pictish Confederation in 685 at the battle of Dunnichen (Nechtansmere), Northumbria began to lose political dominance but blossomed in cultural terms.

Bede had inherited the use of a superbly furnished library and his *Ecclesiastical History of the English People* was a seminal work, one which earned him the sobriquet of 'Father of English History' (1899) and, in his lifetime a doctorate from Pope Pius XIII. A brilliant linguist and translator, his work made a significant contribution to the development of Christianity in England. He wrote on history, theology, music and metrics. His *Historia* is essentially a history of the church and lay events are only introduced to underscore a moral point and while he did not invent the *Anno Domini* method of dating, his use of this ensured its general adoption.

SIR HENRY PERCY ('HOTSPUR') (1364/6–1403)

During his turbulent life and after, Sir Henry Percy came to represent the apogee of chivalry and was regarded as the epitome of knightly virtue, an image Shakespeare reflects in *Henry IV Part I*. Some, however, regard him as an exponent of that unruly brand of magnatial thuggery which characterised the 'overmighty' subject. A son of the 1st Earl (all the Percys, confusingly, are Henrys, so they end up being numbered like royalty), he rose to prominence during the border wars of the late fourteenth century. The Percys did very well from the conflict, buying up manorial holdings at a discount and maintaining an army, at the crown's expense, to resist the resurgent Scots.

This they (and particularly Hotspur) did with great élan. He fought the moonlit battle of Otterburn in August 1388, losing to the earls of March and Douglas, the latter of whom fell in the fight. Advised by the same Scottish earl who'd defected to the English, he scored a notable victory at Homildon thirteen years later but sowed the seeds of his own ruin in a dispute over ransoms with Henry IV. The Percys had acted as kingmakers during the Lancastrian usurpation, abandoning their expressed allegiance to Richard II. This quarrel led to rebellion and a traitor's death at Shrewsbury in 1403. For a while the Percy star was eclipsed. Shrewsbury field was the first fight in which both sides deployed the longbow and casualties were accordingly very high. It was a clothyard shaft which ended Hotspur's career.

SIR JOHN MARLEY (1590–1673)

Marley commanded the Royalist garrison during the epic Civil War siege of 1644. The mayor was a local merchant adventurer, one of the mercantile elite or 'hostmen', so was not strictly a military commission. Gruff old Jacob Astley had been military governor four years earlier and had surrendered the town to Leven's Scottish forces after the debacle of Newburn Ford. The Marquis of Newcastle had conducted the initial stages of the defence in the opening months of 1644 before falling back with his army beneath the walls of York. He emerged upon Rupert's relief to join forces and fight at the calamitous battle of Marston Moor which witnessed the loss of his army and ruin of his cause.

Marley then maintained the hopeless defence through September and into the wet autumn. There was no hope of succour and the odds at best were unfortunate. Marley is perceived as his enemies viewed him, as obstinate and wilful, exposing the townsfolk to further suffering where there was no prospect of deliverance. This was perhaps an unduly pejorative view as the mayor had hopes the Scots, enfeebled by desertions, sickness and general want of stores might have to abandon the siege altogether. The town was stormed and Marley, on his final capitulation, interned with his neck at risk. He escaped, or was allowed to, and returned with Charles II at the Restoration.

TOM TATE

Tom was employed as a gaoler at Newgate. This ancient portal, massive and resilient, survived even the great siege of 1644, although it took a pounding, doubled as it was as a prison. Small chambers set within the great thickness of masonry were handily employed as cells and conditions were by no means as grim as might be imagined. Newgate seems to have been a slightly more enlightened place of incarceration. In June 1736 Tom the turnkey found himself on the wrong side of the bars, he'd indulged in some light fingered extra-mural activities and been caught. One advantage he possessed, of course, was his intimate understanding of his surroundings. He was in fact lodged in a cell adjoining the Great North Road toll house.

This was a boon as Tom was able to arrange for a band of confederates to occupy the toll house while he and another felon, named Ogle, hacked through the crumbling stonework. The noise apparently did not suffice to raise any alarm and the pair were allowed to bash through a tunnel sufficient to permit them to just squeeze through. Their shackles were quickly struck off and the gang were ready to escape. Tom was in a filthy state, his civvies and valuables were stored in the Gaoler's Lodge. Undeterred, relying on his intimacy with the aged structure, Tom succeeded in breaking in this time and retrieving all of his goods and chattels. Then he and Ogle fled. Not that far it has to be said; the pursuit closed in at Bellingham and Tom Tate found himself again in irons, this time bound for the Americas!

JOHN WILSON ('CUCKOO JACK')

The Flying Horse tavern in Newcastle's Groat Market was the haunt of a singular clientele, collectively known as the 'Newcastle Eccentrics'. A fairly motley crew, they were notoriously hard-drinking and rumbustious and were made up of 'Cull Billy', 'Knack-kneed Mack', 'Bugle Nosed Jack' and other desperados tunefully led by Blind Willie Purvis, an accomplished fiddler. None was more colourful or richly Dickensian than John Wilson, better known as 'Cuckoo Jack'. Wilson was a bargeman and knew the river with rare intimacy and his skill in predicting where objects lost overboard might resurface earned him many a commission.

His aptitude as a scavenger was put to particular purpose by the corporation which paid him to recover corpses of victims of drowning and suicides from the sluggish water. Remuneration was per cadaver but those recovered from below the Tyne Bridge were priced more highly than those dredged from above the crossing, the waters here being trickier. Profit is a strong motivator and Jack was known to wait until some poor wretch who had fallen in from the quayside had been washed down into more lucrative shoals. As he was attending to routine chores one day the alarm was raised, 'How Jackie, quick, there's some gadgie [person] fallen in the river!' Wilson's laconic reply was, 'Whey man, hadaway [go away, get away]! Ah get more for a deed 'un. Let the bugger droon [drown]!'

BLACK JACKIE JOHNSON (d. 1837)

The Age of Reason never quite dispelled the fug of antique terrors and mire of superstition that had characterised earlier ages. Late Georgian inhabitants of Newcastle frequently sought the counsel of John Johnson of Dog Bank before committing themselves to a new or hazardous venture. 'Black Jackie' boasted a copy of a celebrated classical necromancer's guide by the great magus Cornelius Agrippa. This was a practitioner's manual to the black arts and very useful it was too.

One of Jackie's specialities was advising unmarried spinsters upon the identity of eligible suitors – a most important business. He could also delve into the world of the subconscious, at least two generations before Freud or Jung. Having a magic mirror helped enormously, so potent was the reputation of this most useful accessory that robbers would return stolen goods merely upon the knowledge their victims had consulted the seer!

Jackie may have done a roaring trade but the city fathers felt this was not the image of Newcastle, as a prosperous up-and-coming industrial hub that they wished to cultivate. Such was the pressure they applied he was obliged to move eastwards beyond their reach to Byker where he continued business as normal until his death in 1837. Even his going off proved worthy of legend – it is said he expired in the very act of dealing tarot and stayed frozen in that pose for several days. In his will he bequeathed the whole of his necromancer's tools and manuals to the people of Newcastle, one has to wonder what became of this very extraordinary bequest.

CHARLES AVISON (1709–70)

Avison was, for most of the time since his death, largely forgotten in his home town, and was not culturally resurrected until the Charles Avison Society was established in the 1990s. He was a native, born to parents who were themselves both musicians and he became a member of the hallowed Incorporated Company of Town Waits (musicians). He was licensed to teach music, his stipend from the corporation was £4 per annum. It would appear that local MP and noted patron of the arts Ralph Jennison encouraged his early works, though Avison certainly spent time in London, studying under the Italian composer Francesco Geminiani. In the mid-1730s he was appointed as organist, firstly at St John's then, a year later, at St Nicholas', where his remuneration was fixed at the yearly figure of £20, a by no means unattractive salary. And of course, he continued to teach:

> Mr. Avison begs to acquaint his friends that Mondays and Fridays are set apart for his teaching in Newcastle. He proposes to attend young ladies on the harpsichord between the hours of nine and one in the forenoon and from two to six in the evening, he will teach the violin and German flute. The terms are half-a-guinea per month (or eight lessons) and one guinea Entrance.

The composer was also much involved in organising concerts and music for the local stage. He remained committed to Newcastle, turning down lucrative offers including that of organist at York Minster and a substantive teaching post in Edinburgh. In January he married Catherine Reynolds, by whom he had nine children (although six of these died in infancy). His national reputation was guaranteed by his *Essay of Musical Expression* of 1752, the first such undertaking in English. He was buried in St Andrew's churchyard where his grave may still be visited.

WILLIAM BEILBY (1740–1819)

Beilby came from a family of craftsmen – his father (also William) worked as a goldsmith and jeweller in Durham, although the family moved to Newcastle after the business collapsed. William senior died some years later as did one of the younger William's brothers. Working alongside his sister Mary (1749–97), William began to specialise as a glass enameller. Sandgate was home to a thriving glass-making industry and, in 1761, William became, probably, the first British craftsman to successfully fire enamels into glass, so that the enamel became essentially an intrinsic element. His elder brother Ralph, who had taken over the established part of the family business, became a noted engraver, working particularly in copper, from 1767 the young Thomas Bewick was apprenticed to him and they collaborated extensively until they had a violent disagreement over authorship in 1797 although they did reconcile (at least partially) three years later.

Mary became a painter in enamels in her own right, taught by William and working from the family premises at Amen Corner. She, and the young Bewick, may have been linked romantically, despite the best efforts of older brother Ralph, but she was debilitated by a stroke in 1774 and such ardour as Thomas might have felt, cooled thereafter. William's reputation grew and commissions flowed; in 1778 the clan moved to London and from there to Scotland where Mary later died. William himself, who was also an accomplished water-colourist, finally died in Hull. The art of the Beilbys was revived in 1973 when the late Jimmy Rush published *The Ingenious Beilbys* (Barrie & Jenkins, London).

THOMAS BEWICK (1753–1828)

Thomas was fourteen when he was apprenticed to Ralph Beilby, he had no formal training in art and had been an indifferent scholar; unquestionably he showed talent for drawing. His family were colliers from Mickley, west of Newcastle, and the lad was educated at a local school in Ovingham. Bewick's particular talent inclined towards engravings on wood. He achieved recognition from the Royal Society in 1775 and was made a partner in the Beilby firm a year later. In 1790 he published *A General History of Quadrupeds* followed between 1797 and 1804 with his masterpiece *The History of British Birds*, published in two volumes focusing respectively upon avian life on land and water. Bewick was himself a keen ornithologist.

Bewick's art was honed by working in harder woods, particularly box, carved against the grain and employing the finer tools of the engraver – fruits of his partnership with Ralph although this turned sour when the two quarrelled. Bewick provided engraved illustrations for other authors including Goldsmith. A lifelong obsession was *Aesop's Fables* and he drew for various editions throughout his career. From 1812 he devoted his labours towards a lavish three-volume set of Aesop which appeared in 1818. Some of the work was carried out by his flourishing school of apprentices with finer touches from the master. The fascination of his art has proved an enduring legacy.

He is unique in having two memorials in the city, a copy of the Chillingham Bull near Forth Lane where he lived and a plaque on the site of his workshop in St Nicholas Yard. Remarkably, Bewick was ahead of his time in his understanding of the unique nature of fingerprints, placing his own next to his signature on his work.

CUTHBERT COLLINGWOOD (1748–1810)

Vice Admiral Collingwood, 1st Baron Collingwood, was a native Novocastrian, educated, like so many of the city's distinguished sons, at the Royal Grammar School before, at the tender age of eleven, going to sea under his cousin Captain (later Admiral) Richard Braithwaite on HMS *Shannon*. Collingwood first saw action fighting with the naval brigade to dislodge American rebels from Bunker Hill in 1775 which earned him his lieutenancy. Two years after, he first met Horatio Nelson on board HMS *Lowestoffe*. Thereafter the careers of the two friends became entwined until their final and fateful partnership off Cape Trafalgar in October 1805. HMS *Sampson* with 64 guns was Collingwood's first ship-of-the-line command and he worked closely with Nelson enforcing a blockade of the West Indies against the US. Collingwood saw further action at the Glorious First of June and again at Cape St Vincent where he commanded HMS *Excellent*. In the interim he found time to marry Sarah Blackett, offspring of the established mercantile family.

Dreary and debilitating blockade duty followed until the decisive encounter at Trafalgar, Collingwood being one of that legendary 'band of brothers' who sailed under Nelson to immortal death and glory. *Royal Sovereign*, Collingwood's flagship, was the first to engage (he'd been raised to rear-admiral in 1799). His ship was furiously beleaguered, disabling the great Spanish vessel *Santa Ana*. When his friend and mentor fell in the moment of his triumph, Collingwood assumed overall command and brought the victory to its full decisive conclusion. Trafalgar was his last and greatest fight. For the last five years of his life, the ageing Collingwood accomplished a series of delicate and important diplomatic missions. His health was failing and he died off Port Mahon on 7 March 1801 – ironically he is better commemorated upon Menorca than on his native Tyneside!

Though he never had the romantic flair of Nelson, nor perhaps that level of tactical genius, he was regarded as his equal in seamanship and flawless in political judgements. He was humane, opposed to the press-gang and flogging, respected and revered by his men. At home Collingwood walked extensively from his home in Morpeth and was remarkable for his habit of planting acorns on his walks, many a Northumbrian oak forms part of an enduring legacy.

GEORGE STEPHENSON (1781–1848)

One of the pioneers of the great industrial surge on Tyneside in the early nineteenth century, Stephenson, followed by his equally able son Robert, stands as a titan. Both his background and achievement mark him as unique. Of humble birth, he followed his father, an engineman, into the pits having very little formal education. His questing intelligence spurred him to learn reading and writing in which he was largely self-taught. He worked with the rudimentary steam engines through a series of collieries in both England and Scotland. In 1814, in the year before Waterloo, he built his first locomotive, employed to shift coal at Killingworth. Aptly, the engine was named *Blucher* in honour of the Swedish general who led the Prussian army.

In the very year of Wellington and Blucher's great victory, Stephenson invented a form of mining safety lamp. Six years later he gained a significant position when appointed as engineer for the new Stockton & Darlington Railway. By 1825 the line was open and a year later he took on the greater challenge of the Liverpool to Manchester line. Perhaps his greatest hour came in 1829 when the railway owners mounted trials at Rainhill to ascertain the most suitable locomotive for hauling heavy loads. The event proved a major crowd puller and Stephenson was the man of the hour when his *Rocket* swept aside its competitors, truly rocketing at up to 36mph.

Rocket guaranteed its creator's immortality and announced the arrival of the Age of Steam. Stephenson was at the cutting edge of a great revolution as hundreds of miles of iron rails transformed the English landscape, dragging a nation into modernity. Rural settlements were hauled from medieval isolation and the manufactured goods of the industrial revolution could be hauled in record times and undreamt of quantities. Stephenson's part in this was formative and ongoing. He became the beacon of steam, working through Britain and the Continent. A man who had not learnt to read and write until near adulthood and from exceedingly modest circumstances, Stephenson debated with the cream of Britain's lawyers at inquiries, moving even the bitterest sceptics with his visionary eloquence.

JOSEPH WILSON SWAN (1828–1914)

One of the most important figures of the nineteenth-century phenomenon that was Newcastle was physicist and chemist Joseph Swan, whose enduring fame and continuing legacy rests upon his invention of the incandescent light bulb. Swan quite literally lit up the world. Gaslight was the first source to dispel the darkness of ages and created constant light, Swan's genius transformed the way we live still further. Though a native of Wearside, Swan became a partner in the firm of Mawson, Swan & Morgan on Grey Street and survived there until 1873. Most of the inventor's experiments, however, were conducted at his home, a house called Underhill on Kells Lane North in Low Fell. His large Victorian conservatory became his laboratory and testing ground.

It was in 1850 that he began work on what would become the incandescent light bulb; the process was tortuous and a full decade elapsed before he had a device suitable for patenting. This prototype was by no means satisfactory and a further fifteen years' work ensued and it was not until 1878 that a further patent was granted. This was roughly a year before Thomas Edison, working in the same field, was able to demonstrate a viable a viable prototype of his own. By 1880 Swan obtained a further patent for his finished product and, fittingly, his own home at Underhill was the first property in England to be lit by electric light.

The Literary and Philosophical Society, perhaps equally fittingly, was the first public space to have the benefit of electric lighting. It was the Savoy Theatre in London which became the first public building of note to be entirely lit by Swan. Honours followed acclaim, Swan was knighted by Edward VII in 1904, awarded the Royal Society's prestigious Hughes Medal. As far back as 1881 he had been awarded the *Legion d'honneur* in Paris, the Parisians lit their great city with Swan's bulbs.

WILLIAM, LORD ARMSTRONG (1810–1900)

Perhaps none of the colossi of Newcastle's industrial age quite bestrode the world stage so largely as William George Armstrong, 1st Baron Armstrong. His father was a successful quayside corn merchant and local politician (mayor in 1850). William was born in Shieldfield and educated privately. Though the young student evinced an interest in engineering and married a factory owner's daughter, he was destined for a career in the law. For eleven years he practised as a solicitor and built a home in Jesmond Dene. His keen eye and naturally inventive bent fuelled a number of early ideas which crystallised into his design for the hydraulic crane, an instant success and Armstrong's designs were soon in action unloading sips along Newcastle's busy Quayside – an inventor was born.

In 1847 Armstrong took the plunge and with backing from his former law partner, set up business as W.G. Armstrong & Co. which began constructing premises at Elswick. Orders came in fast and steady – by 1850 he turned out 50 cranes. Very soon that output was doubled and remained constant for the remainder of the century. His workforce was quickly numbered in hundreds and the firm was soon building bridges as well as cranes. The mid-nineteenth century saw the birth of industrial warfare, mechanised mass killing that would reach its dreadful apogee on the Western Front two generations later. An earlier conflict, the Crimean War and the failures of British gunnery spurred Armstrong to think in terms of improved ordnance.

His breech-loading gun with rifled barrel was to transform the face of battle. By 1855, the prototype five-pounder was ready, soon followed by an eighteen-pounder. Armstrong's gun, which fired shell rather than traditional roundshot, proved superior to all rivals and a politic gift of his patent to the government of the day, ensured both acclaim and reward. He founded a new ordnance factory at Elswick to maintain a nominal impartiality from his sinecure as Engineer of Rifled Ordnance to the War Office. Expansion was swift and exponential. It wasn't long before Armstrong turned his prolific eye upon naval ordnance and by the time of his death his great works employed tens of thousands and provided armaments for half the world. Sadly, its successor in title, BAE Systems, will cease manufacturing operations at Elswick in 2011 bringing a century and a half's tradition of manufacturing excellence to a close.

EMILY WILDING DAVISON (1872–1913)

Deeds not words – the suffragette motto is carved on Emily Davison's grave in St Mary's churchyard in Morpeth, regarded as her home town as her family are from there and she lived in nearby Longhorsley with her mother. Emily was in fact born in London, however, and proved a very accomplished student though her education was cut short when her widowed mother suffered financial constraints. She worked as a teacher in a variety of posts but her fiery zeal for the cause of women's suffrage ensured she was often in trouble with the law.

She quite savagely attacked a man she mistook for Lloyd George, later in 1913, she planted a bomb at the real Lloyd George's house, resulting in extensive damage. In gaol she went on hunger strike and, while in Holloway, was force fed. On the night of 2 April 1911, as the date for the census of that year she hid herself in a cupboard in the Palace of Westminster so that she could properly claim her address at the time as 'House of Commons'. Veteran bandwaggoner Tony Benn later placed a plaque at the location.

Her moment of ambiguous glory came on 4 June 1913, the day of the Derby. As the king's horse Anmer swept around Tattenham Corner, Emily ran out and was struck down. She suffered multiple injuries and died four days later in hospital without giving any account of her motives – the moment was memorably caught on film by Pathé News. It has been suggested that her act was one of deliberate martyrdom, or just plain suicide. It may be she was attempting to pin the WSPU flag to the king's horse, or simply to run across the track waving the flag. In any event her death made her the first suffragette martyr and her funeral became a lavish PR event. Her home town turned out to pay their respects to a lost daughter as the cortege returned to Morpeth. In fact she was not the only victim, jockey Herbert Jones who could have done nothing to avert the tragedy was haunted by Emily thereafter and this may well have contributed to his own suicide in 1951.

ADAM WAKENSHAW VC (1914–42)

June 1942 was not a good time for the Allies. In the Western Desert, Tobruk had fallen and Rommel's victorious Deutsche Afrika Korps was pursuing the 8th Army eastwards towards its final strongpoints running inland from the then unheard of railway halt at El Alamein. Adam Herbert Wakenshaw, a Tyneside labourer, was a private serving in 9th Battalion Durham Light Infantry, part of 151 Brigade. The Durhams were in the thick of it as usual when, at 05.15 on the morning of 21 June, 9th Battalion came under an Axis attack. Wakenshaw, who was mourning the tragic death in an accident of his seven-year-old son, John, was with one of the battalion's two-pounder anti-tank guns. These were light, fast firing and accurate but largely ineffective against German armour which, at this stage, still maintained a significant qualitative superiority.

Quite early in the action a German tracked vehicle towed a light gun to within close range of the two-pounder, sited on a forward slope in front of the infantry positions. The battalion gun crew opened fire and put it out of action with a round through the engine. The Germans replied with another mobile gun and either killed or wounded the men manning the two-pounder. They then moved forward towards the damaged tractor and tried to get the light gun in action against the infantry. Wakenshaw had already lost one arm yet he crawled back to the damaged two-pounder and fired a further five rounds. The German vehicle burst into flames and the gun was damaged. Another German round struck the position, killing the single other survivor and wounding Wakenshaw again. Despite these dreadful injuries, he somehow crawled back to the weapon and managed to insert a sixth and final shell into the chamber just before a further, direct hit killed him. His body was found that evening. For such astonishing gallantry he was awarded a posthumous VC.

SID CHAPLIN (1916–86)

Actually a native of Shildon in Durham, Chaplin was a highly respected local author who worked in the mines during the Second World War. Later, he worked for the NCB magazine and his first, influential novel *The Leaping Lad* was published in 1946. A further four works appeared during the late 1950s and '60s though it was his stage musical *Close the Coalhouse Door* of 1968, written with Alan Plater and Alex Glasgow that secured nationwide recognition. One of his teachers once observed that 'Anyone who can make economics entertaining would be wasting his time on them – I think you should go in for writing!' Sage advice, his OBE was awarded in 1977.

ALAN PLATER (1935–2010)

Plater maintained links with his native Tyneside, though his family moved to Hull while he was very young. He did return to study architecture and what was then King's College (latterly Newcastle University). He did not flourish in his chosen profession and later quipped that, having been called upon to survey a field, a herd of inquisitive swine attempted to eat his tape measure and the experience propelled him into a writing career!

CATHERINE COOKSON (1906–98)

Catherine ('Kate') Ann McMullen was born in Tyne Dock, the illegitimate daughter of a dipsomaniac, though the bulk of her childhood was spent in Jarrow. Much of her later writing was based on personal experience she and only took up the pen as a tool to combat depression. Leaving school at thirteen, Kate worked in domestic service and ran a number of laundries. She suffered from a rare vascular condition and was plagued by a series of miscarriages which brought on a breakdown. Despite all of these barriers, her first novel, *Kate Hannigan*, was published in 1950. She went on to write nearly 100 more and sold more than 123 million copies worldwide, for seventeen years running she was the UK's most borrowed author. Her books formed the basis for a run of radio and TV adaptations – the later were filmed in the region, many episodes making use of the recreated 1913 township at Beamish Open Air Museum.

BASIL BUNTING (1900–85)

Basil Cheesman Bunting published his seminal *Briggflatts* in 1966, a relative latecomer to popular acclaim. A Quaker from Scotswood by birth, he attended the Royal Grammar School though it was his Quaker upbringing which led him to adopt a pacifist stance during the First World War. At the time this required significant moral courage and for his beliefs, he suffered a year in gaol at Wormwood Scrubs and Winchester. A contemporary described him as 'a conservative, anti-fascist imperialist'. Recovering from the rigours of prison he moved to London in the 1920s, then, enjoying the Bohemian vogue, to Paris where he became friendly with Ezra Pound, settling with his family for a spell in Italy.

He spent the Second World War serving with Military Intelligence in Persia and stayed on after the war on the embassy staff until expelled by the regime in 1952. It was thereafter he returned to his native Newcastle working as a journalist on the *Evening Chronicle*. He named his work *Briggflatts* after the Quaker meeting house in Cumbria which hosts his grave, though he actually died in Hexham.

ERIC VICTOR BURDON (1941–)

Eric Victor Burdon, a native of Newcastle, was the founder vocalist in the 1960s group the Animals, one of that select group of British artists which led the UK 'invasion' of the American music scene. Named fifty-seventh in *Rolling Stone* magazine's 'top one hundred best singers of all time', Burdon founded the Animals with Alan Price who was born in Fatfield near Washington, a former student of Jarrow Grammar. Price had founded his own group, the Alan Price Rhythm and Blues Combo, in 1958. Formed in 1962, the Animals split in 1966, reforming again nine years later with a final album being released in 1977. Both Burdon and Price continued with successful solo careers. Perhaps their 'House of the Rising Sun' together with Lindisfarne's 'Fog on the Tyne' are the most successful Tyneside-born tracks from the 1960s and '70s.

GORDON SUMNER (1951–)

'Sting' was born in Wallsend and spent part of his childhood assisting his father with the daily milk round. His most treasured possession was an old Spanish guitar with five rusted strings, left behind by a relative who'd emigrated. He was a pupil at St Cuthbert's Grammar, before a succession of unsatisfactory jobs as bus conductor, labourer and revenue official. From 1971 to 1974 he studied towards a teaching qualification. That was the day job, he taught in Cramlington while performing as a jazz musician in the evenings. Once onstage he appeared in a yellow and black striped jersey which earned him the nickname Sting.

In 1977 he made the move to London where he joined Stewart Copeland and, later, Andy Summers to form the Police. He has throughout his highly influential career incorporated elements of jazz, reggae, classical, new age and worldbeat. He has garnered 16 Grammy awards (the first being in 1981 for Best Rock Instrumental Performance) together with a subsequent Oscar nomination.

MARK KNOPFLER (1949–)

Mark Freuder Knopfler OBE achieved considerable fame and critical acclaim as the lead guitarist, singer and songwriter for the totemic 1980s band, Dire Straits. He created the group with his brother Dave in 1977 and Dire Straits enjoyed enormous sales, over 120 million albums in all before they disbanded in 1995. Knopfler was in fact born in Glasgow; his father was a Hungarian Jewish exile who'd been obliged to flee the Communist regime. As a boy his family settled in Blyth and Mark, together with his brother, attended Gosforth Grammar School.

He began his career as a journalist in Leeds but moved to London where he joined a High Wycombe band Brewer's Droop. Initially the *Dire Straits* album failed to attract much critical notice but the success of the single 'Sultans of Swing' proved a catalyst for the band's meteoric success. Knopfler has also created some memorable film scores including those for *Local Hero, Metroland, Cal, Last Exit to Brooklyn* and *The Princess Bride*. He achieved a first degree in English in his journalism days and now holds three honorary doctorates in music.

JIMMY NAIL (1954–)

Nail, born James Bradford in Benton, achieved recognition in the role of 'Oz' in *Auf Wiedersehen Pet* – even though he had never acted previously aside from an extra's role in *Get Carter*. His first choice was music and he has a long and successful career as a singer/ songwriter behind him. His role as Geordie copper Spender in the series of the same name was followed by his own project *Crocodile Shoes*. Since then he has had significant roles in the film version of *Evita, Still Crazy* and in the film adaptation of Roald Dahl's *Danny, the Champion of the World*.

His attempt to revive *Auf Wiedersehen Pet* in 1999 was highly acclaimed and the series attracted substantial numbers of viewers. His music has also flourished, his album, *Crocodile Shoes* sold over a million copies in 1994.

CHERYL COLE (1983–)

Now an international style icon, Cheryl was born here and raised in the less than desirable Walker area where she attended the local comprehensive. Her academic career was unpromising and she was twice suspended, once for brawling. Her day job as a waitress ended in 2002 when she won a TV reality contest *Popstars the Rivals* with a group of other young women who formed the highly successful Girls Aloud. The band achieved a score of consecutive top ten UK singles and recorded five platinum albums and as many BRIT Awards nominations. The band members went their separate ways in 2008.

Cole was appointed onto the panel of TV judges for the vastly successful *X-Factor* in 2008 and her solo career took off with two top ten UK albums and two no. 1 singles. Her marriage to footballer Ashley Cole proved less satisfactory. However, her face has featured on the front covers of *Vogue, Elle* and *Harper's Bazaar*. Despite her global stardom, she is still every inch a Geordie.

5

MOVEMENT – THE TRANSPORT CONNECTION

RIVER AND PORT

The origins of the name 'Tyne' are unclear; it may derive from *Tin* in a local Celtic dialect and the river might, to the Romans, have been known as the Vedra. What is certain is that the spring rises in North Tynedale and flows down this haunting valley to meet with the South Tyne at their confluence.

The river is at the very core of the town and its enduring prosperity, being significant strategically, commercially and perhaps even spiritually. Newcastle is above all a port and, for centuries, a military base for operations against the Scots. Without this great river, any history of the place would have been entirely different. Along its length flowed arteries of trade and industry – coal in vast quantities, ships, armaments and munitions.

Perhaps the true, unsung heroes of the river are the Tyne Commissioners. Up until the middle years of the nineteenth century much of the waterway was silted up and impossible for navigation; even tiny river steamers frequently grounded. Dredging operations commenced in earnest in 1861 and, by the outbreak of war in 1914, some 133,000,000 tons of waste had been dredged and dumped at sea. In the course of these improvements a whole series of mid-rivers islets became casualties; King's Meadows by rural Elswick, where regattas had long been held, was one of these. Small headlands were also sheared away; Bill Point, Bill Quay, Friar's Goose and Whitehill Point disappeared. Shields harbour was scoured of shoals and, by the Low Lights, where the waters narrowed, more dredging resulted in a widening of the channel to some 670ft across, giving the river the look it retains now. Shallow depths were also dredged out to permit safe passage of larger vessels.

As early as 1854, the commissioners had begun work on the construction of the two great stone piers which thrust outwards into the cold confines of the wild North Sea, providing their key achievement after dredging. Work was not completed until some forty years after. Perhaps the most significant milestone further upstream was the opening of Armstrong's ingenious Swing Bridge in 1876. Prior to this the waters beyond the old stone bridge had remained shallow and somnolent; locals were easily able to wade into the sluggish stream to collect waste and salvage. Once the new bridge, swung on hydraulic rams, opened access to the channel beyond, more dredging work was undertaken. An existing lazy bend at Lemington was excised by the cutting of a new link which reduced the gap between Scotswood and Newburn by ¾ of a mile. These were far reaching changes, only now could Armstrong's great gun works flourish and quantities of 'King Coal' be shipped from Dunston and Derwenthaugh Staithes.

THE NEW QUAY

With the river dredged, widened and the channel deepened, the old quay began to look distinctly unstable, so the corporation took on the task of rebuilding, beginning in 1864 with work continuing for the better part of two decades. This grand new construction extended for practically a full mile, all the way from Swing Bridge on the west to Ouseburn in the east. The port thrived; pleasure steamers and packets departed for London and continental havens, cattle and produce were landed with a great grain silo rising like a monolith. Armstrong's hydraulic cranes swung loads incessantly served by a rail connection. Every half an hour small steamers crossed the river to Shields and, on the hour, 'above-bridge' to Elswick.

Change sounded a death knell for the keelmen (see pp. 88–9) and the steady swelling of busy Tyne traffic necessitated the construction of enclosed dock areas. In 1857, the Duke of Northumberland officially opened Northumberland Dock which covered some 50 acres between

Howdon and North Shields. A full generation later and the future King Edward VII performed a similar function to unveil the 22¼ acres of Albert Edward Dock. Two years after the opening of Northumberland Dock, North Eastern Railway Company cut the tape on Tyne Dock, a further 50 acres over Jarrow Slake. Latterly, more of the former Slake was absorbed into new timber ponds and, in 1884, the commissioners assumed responsibility for lighting the booming waters from Trinity House.

One of the driving forces behind the tireless work of the commissioners was Joseph Cowen, who chaired the commission for twenty years from 1853 until his death. An artisan who had been politically active since his youth, he built a fortune making bricks at Blaydon, and served as an MP for two terms, elected first in 1865 and again three years later. He'd protested against the infamous Peterloo Massacre, agitated against the Corn Laws and his memory was preserved for decades with the building named after him and which latterly housed the University of Newcastle's adult education department.

THOSE BRIDGES

Our bridges really define the city: had the Roman name lingered we would still be named after one. The first was given the family name of the emperor who ordered it built: Hadrian was an Aelian, hence *Pons Aelius*. It survived from around AD 122 until the tempest of 1248.

The Georgian bridge was less successful. Its broad piers took up a third of the river, dangerously concentrating the currents to render the water impossible to navigate at times. By 1866, demand for more room saw it demolished to make way for construction of the marvellous engineering of the Swing Bridge.

Lord Armstrong arranged for the construction of the hydraulically powered bridge to provide access to his massive weapons factory. The great inventor wanted to make room for larger ships to pass up river so came up with a design that could be moved to make room for river traffic. Electric pumps force water into a 60ft underwater shaft. Releasing it under pressure operates the machinery which swings the bridge aside as needed. The engineering used today is that installed by Armstrong – still going strong.

For those long centuries from the coming of Rome until the Age of Steam, a single river crossing sufficed. Battered, repaired and finally replaced, the Tyne Bridge served its purpose admirably. It is perhaps surprising then that people's most common perception of Newcastle is the great panorama of the Tyne Bridges, each majestic and distinguished in its own right, now complemented by the addition of the new Millennium Bridge.

HIGH LEVEL

Robert Stephenson's masterpiece, the High Level, was one of the first of its kind – a wrought iron tied arch, designed to complete the London–Edinburgh line for the York, Newcastle & Berwick Railway Company. Opened in 1850 it cost some £491,000. The official opening was celebrated by a local man jumping from a parapet into the river. He bet a quart of beer on his survival which, happily, he lived to drink.

The bridge is said to have 'vibrated like a piece of thin wire' during the great fire of Newcastle and experienced one or two structural problems. For starters, trains wanting to go south after terminating at Newcastle had to reverse out of the station, while trains for Edinburgh had to swap to the locomotive at the other end to continue. Cracks were found in some of the iron girders when the bridge was closed for maintenance in 2005. As a result it now carries only bus, taxi and pedestrian traffic.

REDHEUGH BRIDGE

Thomas Bouch, whose name and reputation are forever linked with the Tay Bridge Disaster, was responsible for the Redheugh Bridge, the unlucky bridge. The current version (number three) was designed to withstand the impact of a 10,000-ton ship going at 5 knots. Hopefully this will never happen, especially since it is a long time since a ship that big made it up river. You can understand the concern. Construction of the first bridge (1871) was plagued by delays caused by poor access roads and lack of skilled labour. Structural faults emerged by 1885. That was longer than the life of its sister bridge, also designed by Sir Thomas Bouch, which collapsed in 1879!

It was cheaper to build a replacement which opened in 1907. Sounds good, until you recall that work started ten years earlier. There was no lack of serious ingenuity – hydraulic jacks were used to bump the superstructure along until it rested on the piers of the previous construction but, yet again, they had trouble finding skilled labour and the right materials.

By the 1960s serious design flaws once again became apparent. Speed restrictions of 10mph and weight reductions limited traffic, it became clear it would be cheaper to start again rather than attempt repairs. A friend recalls a discussion with one of the engineers who went out to do some of the last structural checks. He and his companions were rigorous in examining both ends of the bridge: they just did not cross the centre of it to do so.

TYNE BRIDGE

The symbol of Newcastle for a host of people, it was opened in 1928 although it was first proposed in 1864 by those fed up with the high tolls on the High Level. It only became possible in the 1920s when central government funding became available and required the passing of a dedicated Act of Parliament (the Newcastle upon Tyne and Gateshead (Corporations) Bridge Act). Costing £1.2 million, it took four years to build. The towers were intended to provide five storeys of warehousing with lifts to take foot passengers from quayside to roadway. Somebody seemingly forgot to put floors in so it was never used for commercial purpose, although the lifts did go in and were used right up to the last years of the twentieth century. There was a suggestion in the 1990s that the work be completed and the towers turned into nightclubs.

Trams ran across the bridge until 1950 and at one point it carried the A1 across the river. 1,000 balloons were released to celebrate its anniversary in 1978.

The engineers were Dorman Long, following designs from Mott, Hay and Anderson. Clients were both corporations, Newcastle and Gateshead, together with the Department of Transport. On each side of the river, elegant but massive concrete towers provide anchors for the sweeping triumph of steel archway that carries the carriageway suspended below. For over eighty years, this epic span has defined our view of the city, shifting the axis away from the railways onto the roads. These five, now six, fine bridges are not the only crossings, as two more have been erected at Scotswood, a suspension bridge from 1831 and a railway bridge, forty years later.

OTHER BRIDGES

Which was the last bridge over the Tyne to charge a toll? Why, the little one at Newburn of course; it only ceased to do so in 1947 when it was taken over by the County Council.

In 1906, King Edward VII returned to unveil the bridge that bears his name, constructed for North Eastern Railways by the highly successful and prolific Cleveland Bridge Company which was, in its long history, responsible for some of the world's greatest spans including the mighty Bosphorus Bridge.

THOSE KEELMEN

In the pantheon of figures unique to Newcastle, a breed as distinctive (and often as contentious) as the reivers were the keelmen. A 'keel' was a form of fat bellied, single-masted, open longboat, oval in shape and purpose-built for the sole job of ferrying coals. Both keels and keelmen were spawned by King Coal and the tradition endured for centuries until dredging and maritime expansion in the mid-nineteenth century did away with them and their trade passed into history and legend.

The author has a connection with this remarkable race as his own great-great-great-grandfather and several known generations beforehand worked as keelmen. Typically the boat was crewed by the master, two seamen and a junior, known as the 'pee-dee'. Though essentially, inshore their trade demanded both strength and seamanship. They rowed their laden vessels, each groaning under around 20 tons of coal, out to colliers waiting in the deeper channel. Each cargo had to be loaded and unloaded by hand, back-breaking work, pace dictated by the ebb and swell of the tide and omnipresent commercial imperative.

They were a breed and a class apart, as distinctive as Nelson's tars, their dress a gaudy yellow waistcoat, short, blue reefer jacket and jaunty straw boater. Theirs was a hard life, rigorous and exposed to the elements in all their mercurial ferocity. Keelmen were not noted for gentility or refinement, nor for religious observance, yet a further affront to bourgeois sensibilities in a pious age. John Wesley, who secured many converts in the north through his tireless eloquence, failed to make an impression to the extent that he was very nearly ducked in the river. The outraged preacher was saved from manhandling by at least one convert, Mrs Bailes the fishwife, a lady not to be argued with. This formidable matron embraced the good cleric in a maternal hug while brandishing her gleaming blade at the muttering mob: 'If ony yen o'lift up anithor hand for to touch ma canny man, ayl floor ye directly.' The keelmen knew sufficient about Mrs Bailes to take the hint!

BACK ONTO THE STREETS

Although Tynesiders are said to have been christened 'Geordies' after their support for George I, a mere nine years after the Guildhall Riots described in Chapter 1, the keelmen took to the streets once again. This time they marched as far west as Elswick to protest against George II, openly espousing the failed cause of the exiled Charles Stuart. This was probably more in jest than expectation but clearly demonstrates their natural resistance to authority, local or even royal. Substantial rewards were offered to identify those responsible. Sedition was a most serious matter and retribution was likely to be dire. The threat from the defeated Stuarts was still perceived to be sufficiently real to cause ripples of alarm in Whitehall but keelmen formed their own tight-knit circle and no takers could be found.

> As aa cam' thro' Sandgate,
> Thro' Sandgate, thro' Sandgate,
> As aa cam' thro' Sandgate'
> Aa heard a lassie sing:
> Weel may the keel row,
> The keel row, the keel row
> Weel may the keel row
> That ma laddie's in.
> He wears a blue bonnet,
> Blue bonnet, blue bonnet,
> He wears a blue bonnet,
> An' a dimple on his chin.
> An' weel may the keel row . . . etc.
>   *'The Keelrow'*

PRESS-GANGED!

Obviously the hostmen in earlier days and their successors, the coal barons, needed the keelmen – their specialist skills were an integral and essential element in the overall prosperity of this staple industry.

One man who was to have a direct influence was Napoleon Bonaparte whose adventures and growing menace fuelled the rapid expansion of the Georgian Navy. Nelson's 'Band of Brothers' needed skilled seamen to man Men o' War and none in the civilian sector were better qualified than Newcastle's keelmen, whose expressed enthusiasm for brawling added allure. Skilled bruisers were just what their Lordships of the Admiralty were seeking.

Efforts at voluntary enlistment foundered largely without trace, the life of a jack tar had little to commend it, nasty, poor, brutal and very often distressingly short.

Newcastle Law Courts now cover ground once occupied by the Plough Inn on what was Spicer Chare. It was here the Crown's representatives set up their campaign HQ. If voluntary enlistment failed to entice then King George would rely on more coercive means – the dreaded press-gang! Their tactics were far from subtle and keelmen whose reputation for hard-drinking was entirely gained through diligent application, left themselves vulnerable if they lingered too long over the last pint. Informers would notify the press where such ale-soaked victims might be found and the mark would be enticed with a further jug. Too befuddled to refuse, the keelman might not notice a king's shilling dropped into his brimming cup. Blissfully unaware he'd just volunteered, the victim would stagger outside into the capable arms of the press, and a life on the ocean wave for the duration awaited. Unsurprisingly, the system didn't allow for appeals.

Families would find their man had simply disappeared en route to Portsmouth and uncertain, often brief servitude on a Man o' War. So great was the resulting hardship that from 1796 the poor rate was increased to 6s in the pound. Such disruption incurred the hostility of the coal traders who sought to restrict any help the corporation might offer to the detested press. Keelmen were quick to adopt cunning expedients to keep drinking of course but minimise the risk of entrapment, thus the glass bottomed tankard to reveal the fatal shilling. If a man was daft enough to be taken, the press might find themselves assailed from all sides by his fellows and dependants. Here the wily Tynesiders possessed the inestimable advantage of ground, knowing every deceptive inch of tortuous alleys and chares.

> They've prest my dear Johnny,
> Sae sprightly and sae bonny,
> Alas I shall never more dae weel O.
> The kidnapping squad
> Laid hold o' my lad,
> As he was unloading the keel O
>   *'The Sandgate Lassie's Lament'*

One unlucky local, having fallen into the hands of the press made a break on the Quayside then, as the hounds closed in, leapt into the water. He dodged the Navy but not Father Tyne whose dangerous currents bore him down. One victim was able to claim immunity as a US citizen and had to be put ashore. A local, equally unwilling and observing this near-miraculous deliverance, tried to emulate the accent but 'Lerr'us off an'all, canny lad, ahm a Yankee tae' didn't quite succeed. Sometimes full-scale brawls between press and keelmen broke out. The Navy men, if bested, were in for a savage hiding, humiliated and their officers made to 'ride the steng' a manner of ducking stool lashed to which the luckless midshipman would 'be carried through the streets, exposed to the insults and assaults of an enraged populace, the women in particular bedaubing them plentifully with dirt, etc.' Peace in 1815, as the echoes of Waterloo subsided, might have heralded a return to pre-war employment and boom. It did not; apart from the satisfaction of settling old scores with informers, the keelmen found themselves in a changing world.

THE LONG STOP

As the keelmen's monopoly began to decline, they resorted to what would now be termed industrial action. In October 1822 a bitter dispute, known as 'the long stop' erupted. Now the old alliance between coal magnates and keelmen was fractured as the usefulness of the latter diminished, common purpose was ousted by deep enmity. Both sides sought allies. For their part the keelmen were able to enlist the support of their fellow seafarers crewing colliers while the bosses sought the help of fellow magnates and the armed forces. Tension escalated to such a level that HMS *Swan* was anchored off Sandgate with her guns run out!

As in the old days of the Civil War, London faced a winter without coals; an alliance between keelmen and colliermen effectively closed down traffic and blockaded the river for good measure. Frantic coal-agents in the cold capital were already looking for alternative sources of supply. Nonetheless, both time and technology were against the strikers. Thomas Hedley's steam engine *Thomas and Jeremiah* (inevitably known as *Tom and Jerry*) was converted to maritime use – steam engines were already being used to pull the heavy chaldrons.

On 2 November *Tom and Jerry* took to the river, towing a slew of laden barges, a direct provocation.

Maddened by the affront, strikers chucked stones, a regular fusillade, at the craft and pelted its red-coated minders with slime. Technology might have spurred the challenge but it wasn't necessarily up to delivery. The engine's improvised conversion and the huge weight it was pulling led to frequent stoppages. As soon as the tug faltered, keelmen would wade out and try to tip the barges. Despite *Tom and Jerry*'s best efforts, a mere trickle of coal was making it out of the river, barely 50 tons per day as against a normal 2,250 tons. Hunger, however, proved a powerful ally and, by the first week in December, the strike fizzled out and keelmen grudgingly returned to work, having gained nothing from their action.

This defeat had consequences; failure of industrial action meant construction of new staithes could proceed uninterrupted and the keelmen's livelihood progressively declined. Finally, only the 'above bridge' collieries remained to them and, with the opening of Armstrong's Swing Bridge in 1876, this final bastion was eroded and the keelmen, economically extinct, passed into history.

BY ROAD

I went to Blaydon races t'was on the ninth of June
Eighteen hundred and sixty two on a summer's afternoon
I took the bus from Balmbras and she was heavy laden
Away we went along Collingwood Street to see the Blaydon races

Chorus

Oh me lads, you should've seen us gannin'
Passing the folks along the road just to see them stannin'
All the lads and lasses there all with smilin' faces
Gannin along the Scotswood Road – to see the Blaydon races
'Blaydon Races'

One of the features of West Coast American cities such as Los Angeles, which tends to make a strong impression with visitors from the old world, is the manner in which the city blocks are laid out for the greater convenience of the motorist. The notion of cities that came of age only with internal combustion and where the automobile has equivalent status with the family arsenal is largely alien to us. Newcastle, like most British settlements, grew from Roman through medieval times with motor vehicles entering the picture very late indeed. Our city mushroomed from the river, spreading organically northwards and swelling both east and west along its banks, for long centuries a warren of alleyways and chares. Most expansion and development took place prior to 1900 with the impact of railways leaving most visible scars.

From the inter-war years, as the Age of Steam declined and withered, internal combustion took over and ever increasing demand led to a series of largely ad hoc solutions which have combined to create the current pastiche where brutalist modern highways slash ugly streams through ancient thoroughfares with as much sympathy for historic roots as the trains a century and more beforehand.

Writing in the now distant postwar period, the historian S. Middlebrook observed:

> The increasing integration of industrial Tyneside as the
> metropolitan core of the whole north-east coast area has
> made a system of communications more adequate to present
> requirements essential. Perhaps the chief need is for two new trunk
> roads running north and south, to bypass the most congested
> urban stretch on the river . . . Newcastle as the largest centre
> of population and as the point in which all the chief roads and
> railway lines converge presents an especially difficult problem.
> For the modern city has become much more than the commercial
> capital of the north-east; it is at once a clogged channel through
> which a vast stream of people has to force a passage at peak hours
> from home to work and back again, and the chief shopping and
> entertainment centre not only for the whole of Tyneside but for a
> wide rural hinterland reaching back into two counties.

OVER AND UNDER

This description, penned some six decades ago, could equally apply today. Since then attempts have been made to realise the aspirations expressed in Middlebrook's superb history; two great new arterial highways running east and west of the urban sprawl to channel road traffic away from the centre. To the east, the Tyne Tunnel carries the A19 northwards to its junction with the A1 at Seaton Burn. The tunnel was a significant engineering achievement but crucially flawed in that it is single lane only in both directions. In those threescore years the volume of motor traffic has increased beyond worst nightmare predictions and the single lane tunnel has become, at peak times, a major bottleneck.

A second transport solution, the A1 Western Bypass, has become, also at busy times, and most times between, a veritable traveller's nightmare, Tyneside's very own scaled-down version of the M25 and just about as user-friendly. Those unfortunate enough to traverse this causeway of despair on a daily basis note each dismal landmark as they crawl from one well-remembered milestone to the next. Highlight of the daily tour on the Gateshead side, rising some 20 metres from its grassy knoll and extending its russet steel wings, stands Anthony Gormley's 'Angel of the North'. This totemic sculpture overlooks the habitual gridlock of the A1 and the A167 which follows the line of the old Great North Road through Low Fell towards the Tyne Bridge. Controversial when it was unveiled in 1998, and subject to much local criticism, the statue has gained in status and is accepted as the iconic gateway to Tyneside even as 'an icon of England' – though this may be going a bit far.

THE GREAT NORTH ROAD

And then there was the Great North Road (now the A1/A1M). Expansion in highways provision is not a purely twentieth-century solution, that huge uplift in movement of goods and materials occasioned by the industrial revolution necessitated the first surge in road building towards the latter part of the eighteenth century. By 1815 a series of arterial turnpike roads sprang outwards from Newcastle like spokes of a hub. Wade's crowning achievement, the Military Road, kept pace with Hadrian's earlier efforts westwards through Greenhead to Carlisle. Similar networks spread outwards from Durham and

Darlington but it was the Great North Road which provided the principal north–south artery from the capital through both Durham and Darlington to Newcastle, then northwards again to Berwick upon Tweed and the Scottish border, through Lothian to Edinburgh.

A government postal service was established as early as 1635 and it was this which necessitated a sound transport connection between King Charles' English and Scottish capitals. This route was 'to run night and day between Edinburgh and the City of London, to go hither and come back again in six days conveying all such letters as shall be directed to any post town in the said road . . . and to pay 2*d* for every single letter under four score miles, and if 140 miles, 4*d*, and if above, then 6*d*.'

The highway traditionally kept to the lower and safer coastal plain for those wild reaches of Redesdale and Tynedale were still regarded as bandit country, where denizens had not entirely forgotten the light-fingered ways of their reiver forbears. Grey remarks that, every year, some 20 or 30 of these dalesmen were dragged to the assizes at Newcastle and from there to a rope's end. Coach travellers, looking westwards, would see the great hump of Cheviot, lowering above, 'a landmark for seamen that come out of the east parts from Danzig through the Baltic Sea and from the King of Denmark's country; it being the first land that mariners make for the coast of England.'

From 1786 regular mail coaches began to run from Newcastle, north and south to both capital cities: 'The pace required by the post office at the establishment of the mail coach to Edinburgh was seven miles an hour, and no innkeeper in the town could be found to contract for a speed considered so ruinous for horseflesh, except the landlord of "the Cock Inn" at the head of the Side.' For a substantial fare of 4 guineas, the coach traveller could be transported to London, via Leeds in 45 hours, weather and highwaymen permitting!

CITY STREETS

In terms of the fusion of interest between the heritage needs of an ancient centre and the demands of modern living, centred upon internal combustion, Newcastle represents a particularly unhappy compromise. Since Middlebrook wrote in the early 1950s, a series of expedients has been put in place to alleviate growing pressure from road traffic. In the iconoclastic 1960s and '70s, tarmac was king and heritage took a beating. The central motorway links the Tyne Bridge to Cowgate, one of Newcastle's least alluring suburbs, nursery of urban deprivation, degradation and any illicit substance you care to name. Driven through the heart of the city, here is urban vandalism on a truly epic scale hacking through the core without remorse. The central motorway has joyfully destroyed the prior and pleasing harmony of Jesmond Road and Haymarket. John Dobson Street, a lesser but equally strident outrage, runs parallel to Northumberland Street, its crowning glory a tower block of monstrous incongruity and stark ugliness.

Newcastle's war memorial in the Haymarket. The Northumberland Fusiliers fielded over fifty battalions during the First World War – many thousands did not return.

More recently, Blenheim Street, linking south towards the Western Bypass, has been remodelled with particular savagery, driving a demarcation line between the western fringe of the city centre and Westgate Road, effectively cutting the latter off from any hope of much-needed regeneration. A great deal of new building has taken place in this sector, some of it good, some of it mediocre and a great deal just plain awful; Government Office North East is presently housed in a vast grey monolith of unappealing drabness which manages, against all odds, to look even worse than the buildings which it replaced.

THE 'COFFINS'

This writer is, regrettably, old enough to remember the city's trolley buses. These hybrids were introduced in the autumn of 1935 to replace the earlier tram system. Between then and the outbreak of war, a hundred or so vehicles had come into service. In the aftermath of conflict, austerity notwithstanding, a new fleet 186-strong was commissioned to facilitate an expansion of the system to its greatest length of 37 route miles. The fleet was to comprise 100 three-axle types with the remainder having two. B.U.T. and Sunbeam built the chassis with English Electric and Vickers supplying power; Metro-Cammell and Northern Coach Builders constructed bodywork. Dubbed 'coffins' by drivers due to their relative narrowness, trolley buses remained a vibrant feature of the city's streets until the last were withdrawn on 30 May 1965, being replaced by modern motor buses. Of all that ran, only Newcastle 501, preserved currently at Beamish, remains.

But there was something about the trolley buses. Travelling on one was an altogether different experience. The narrow vehicles, standing somewhere in time between Edwardian trams and diesel Atlanteans, glided and clanked, linked by their own umbilical to overhead electricity supply. When you reached city limits the service ended, as though some ritual passage between town and county had taken place, a clear divide between urban and rural. I journeyed from town out to the uncharted wilds of Fawdon where relatives lived along a farm track, and alighting from the trolley bus proved a significant step in the journey. The walk along a narrow, rutted lane felt like entering new and strange territory. Modern buses are faster and more efficient, freed from the constraints of overhead supply but it's not quite the same – no adventure!

THE RAILWAY KING

Though situated some 60 miles north of Newcastle, spanning the Tweed at Berwick, one of the most enduring monuments to the Age of Steam is the Royal Border Bridge whose sweeping elegance and lofty arches combine function and form in a most eloquent statement. Opened in 1850, it was the largest stone viaduct in Britain. In Newcastle the High Level was virtually contemporary, over 5,000 tons of cast iron was sourced from local foundries and Stephenson's great span required little or no maintenance for a full century and more. Dobson's grand design for the new Central railway station completed the picture. Both this and the Border Bridge were opened in August 1850 by Queen Victoria. Even if Her Majesty was not amused, hopefully she was impressed.

One of those local entrepreneurs most associated with the growth of railways was George Hudson – 'the Railway King'. Hudson was instrumental in consolidating the rather ad hoc local networks into larger and more efficient companies. The 1840s and early 1850s witnessed a fabulous boom in railway expansion. The dynamic of steam transformed the face of England and of the north-east region. A hotchpotch of local tracks and rather dismal, mud-slaked, deeply rutted highways was overtaken by a gleaming web of iron rails that shrank distances, transported large number of passengers and goods over great distances in previously undreamed-of times. Steam was the perfect medium for industrial expansion, fed by ready and eager sources of capital.

Hudson managed to fuse the various local providers into a series of coherent networks by 1854; the York, Newcastle & Berwick Railway, the York & North Midland and Leeds Northern were brought under one corporate banner as the North Eastern Railway Company. Rail changed the face of Newcastle, the Age of Steam ensured the city's dominance as regional hub, a position Newcastle has never surrendered. Steam was the perfect partner for heavy industry, creating a great enterprise in itself; it provided the means to move products the factories were producing. Newcastle's cityscape was also radically altered; the line running from the east into Central station slashed across the historic perspective with the contempt of a new heroic age. That traditional aspect of a city which sprang from the banks of its river and then flowed uphill with the squat majesty of a great square keep was drastically changed, the old no longer mattered.

TORNADO

It is perhaps one of history's ironies that both the age of swords and Age of Steam are relegated to heritage. A vibrant echo of the latter, no. 60163 *Tornado*, a magnificent, fully operational replica of the 'Peppercorn' class A1 locomotives, the last of which was scrapped in 1966, has been built in the region. These were so named after their creator, Arthur Peppercorn, who was the chief engineer for the London & North Eastern Railway. The advent of diesel locomotives heralded their demise but, through their time in service during post-war austerity, their robust, low-maintenance construction proved economical and durable. The iconoclasm of the 1960s, another bright new era, scorned preservation even of the last survivor. Over a span of very nearly twenty years, a dedicated, highly skilled team of enthusiasts laboured to resurrect *Tornado* and the superb new engine took to the rails in 2008; a project which sceptics had dubbed an impossible dream!

TYNE AND WEAR METRO

As a boy, I used to ride the trains from my family home in Longbenton down to the coast, Monkseaton, Whitley Bay and Tynemouth. That was and remains an overland service; such suburban networks were, in part, a Tyneside creation. The Newcastle & North Shields Railway (from Chillingham Road to North Shields) and its counterpart Brandling Junction Railway (Gateshead to Monkwearmouth) are among the oldest of the world's urban systems. Furthermore, the lines were part of the world's very first electric network from 1904.

Developing into a youthful romantic, caught in the lure of trains, one tended perhaps not to notice the shabbiness of rolling stock but, in those halcyon days, stations still had uniformed staff with flower boxes and fading echoes of Edwardian pride. The trains rattled east towards the coast beneath wide skies and a largely level plain where the gaunt colliery towers still stood, though mostly, by this point, idle. The ground was a patchwork of fields with huddled mining settlements (like Backworth and Earsdon) before much of these innocuous flatlands were subsumed beneath a sprawl of uniformly drab executive dwellings.

Newcastle has, since its opening in 1980, enjoyed one of the only two urban underground systems outside London – the Metro, operated by Nexus. This 48-mile network harnessed the existing overground railway alignments which were linked by an ambitious and taxing labyrinth of purpose-built tunnels dug beneath both Newcastle and Gateshead. Metro is big business, current annualised receipts from passenger fares stand at around £40 million with a further 40 million passenger journeys. The network is defined as 'Britain's first modern light railway system, combining light rail, heavy underground metro, high-speed suburban and interurban railway systems.' It is the first in the UK to have installed repeaters, allowing passengers to use their mobiles within the confines of tunnels – Geordie needs his mobile as he needs his very lifeblood!

GOING UNDERGROUND

Part of the engineering challenge in digging the underground links was the extent of former mining tunnels already extant beneath the city, which had to be mapped and, in some cases filled in. One of the most distinctive of these surviving elements, of which Ouseburn Heritage Trust have refurbished as a visitor attraction, is the Victoria Tunnel. This enjoyed a heyday from 1842 until 1860 when it formed an underground waggonway for the movement of coals from Spital Tongues, which lies just north-west of the city centre, to Ouseburn. It enjoyed a further lease of life in the Second World War when, at a hefty cost of £37,000, the subterranean space was recommissioned as an air raid shelter, with accommodation for some 9,000 people.

Commissioned art installations are a feature of the Metro. Since April 2007 artist Nayan Kulkarni's *Nocturne*, a kaleidoscope of moving light images, plays along the Queen Elizabeth II Bridge which carries the

Metro between Newcastle and Gateshead. As an element in Newcastle's ultimately failed bid to win European Capital of Culture in 2008, Michael Pinsky was commissioned to provide Latin signage and a map of Emperor Hadrian's Great Wall within Wallsend station, thus linking two millennia of history (Roman Segedunum lies close by the station).

BY AIR

Some years ago, the writer, an infrequent and not necessarily enthusiastic flyer, took off in a single-seater aircraft from the Newcastle Aero Club which occupied the site of the original aerodrome. The place had a very distinct pre-war feel to it, a mix of Agatha Christie and Indiana Jones. The flight itself was less inspiring, my principal and overriding emotion being a mix of stark terror and nauseous misery. My late uncle, pilot and owner, had kindly offered to take me up for some aerial photography. I was writing on Northumbrian castles at this point and a bird's eye view of locations seemed like a good idea. It wasn't. I'd not been up in a small aircraft before and any *Biggles* or *Blue Max* fantasies were quickly dispelled by some savagely mercurial turbulence and the unheralded rush of RAF jets, not obliged to file flight plans and keen to assert their prominence as kings of the skies. I believe I did kneel to kiss the tarmac when we finally touched down!

Newcastle Airport was originally opened on 26 July, 1935 by the then Secretary of State for Air, Sir Philip Cunliffe-Lister. The site had cost the sum of £35,000 to develop and comprised a relatively modest collection of buildings, clubhouse, hangar, workshops, fuel storage and a grass strip. This early era of passenger aviation still had an aura of romance when air travel was a gentlemanly pursuit untrammelled by the dire levelling of mass package holidays. The Second World War interrupted civilian traffic but a former fighter pilot, Jim Denyer, took over during the heady days of the 1950s when the surging post-war boom was gathering momentum. Destinations were relatively modest, Jersey or the Channel Islands practically qualified as long-haul and passenger numbers did not exceed 5,000.

This would change; a burgeoning tourism industry which kicked off in the 1960s transformed air travel and new runways, air traffic control tower and facilities were unveiled by Harold Wilson. Within a decade passenger numbers had leapt to over a million a year and Newcastle became a regional international airport. Significant investment followed, new check in, catering and retail spaces; in 1991 the Metro was extended out to the airport linking to both regional conurbations. Another Prime Minister, Tony Blair, opened a £27 million extension in the millennium year. Local airline Gill Aviation did not survive long into the new century but a succession of budget airlines have commenced flights, spurring a further, major phase of investment which went into service in summer 2004 and boasted the nation's first self-service kiosks. Two years later some 5.4 million passengers passed through, though the deepening recession has since virtually halved that grand total.

6

CITY OF COMMERCE & CULTURE

THE OLDEST DRUG

What is the oldest drug still in use? Well, it's HRT of course. George Murray was born in Newcastle in 1865 and is credited with the first successful hormone replacement therapy. This involved injecting a patient with an extract of sheep thyroid. His creation is thus reputed to be the oldest drug. He had the Chair of Comparative Pathology at Durham University and practised as a physician at the Royal Victoria Infirmary, while living in Saville Place in Newcastle.

GLASS – WHY CHAMPAGNE IS A GEORDIE DRINK

Sir Robert Mansell, Admiral of the Fleet, was granted a Royal Monopoly for the making of glass in 1623. Newcastle was the logical location for such an activity – coal would fuel the furnaces far better than timber. French Huguenots fleeing their native land in the aftermath of the notorious Massacre of St Bartholomew in 1572 set up businesses alongside the Ouseburn and Skinnerburn but relocated elsewhere when their market declined. Sir Robert and Lady Mansell (both rather forceful characters) drew them back to Newcastle. Just as well, their trade was important. During the Scottish occupation in 1640, a smuggled letter from the mayor referred to his concerns not, as you might perhaps expect, about coal, but over 1,200 cases of precious glassware, ready to be shipped south to London.

A second migration, this time from Italy, was spearheaded by the Dagnia dynasty from Venice, via the Forest of Dean, who arrived here in 1684. By the dawn of the eighteenth century, Newcastle had become the largest glass-producing centre in the world, boasting some 31 glasshouses within half a mile of the town centre (increasing yet further to 41 by 1827). In 1703 Neve wrote of Newcastle: ''tis the glass that is most in use here in England . . . the cases are brought to London in the coal ships.'

When champagne was invented by the celebrated Dom Perignon, he sent for bottles from Newcastle, which he judged to be the best for containing the pressure of his new wine. It did not last; by 1743 – the same year that George II became the last King of England to lead his army personally into battle at Dettingen – 15 tons of glass was exported to Europe, the West Indies and Africa – but none it seems, to France. It might have been different if King George had lost the battle!

By the end of the eighteenth century those 'ingenious' Beilbys were producing Newcastle Light Baluster, examples of which can be viewed in the Rijksmuseum, the Victoria & Albert and other great museums worldwide. Balusters are, in fact, tall glasses with multi-topped stems, often filled with bubbles and white metal. The glass industry moved away into other parts of Tyneside during the nineteenth century. Almost the only memorial now remaining is the Lemington Cone, a notable eighteenth-century firing structure containing no less than 1,750,000 bricks.

TIME OFF FOR GOOD BEHAVIOUR

At the Newcastle Police Court yesterday Michael Dixon, 16 years of age, an apprentice smith at Sir William Armstrong and Co's Works was sent to goal for fourteen days, for absenting himself from his work without leave on 23rd December, this being his second offence.

Newcastle Daily Chronicle, Tuesday 21 January 1873

EARLY RECYCLING

Domestos bleach was invented in a Tyneside garden shed. Wilf and Ivy Handly developed their remarkable product as a combined drain cleaner and treatment for sore feet in 1929. It was sold door-to-door in stoneware jars that were refilled by cyclists from specially designed handcarts. The chemical was employed as treatment for burns during the Second World War. Wilf and Ivy manufactured their bleach from a factory in the Ouseburn Valley that is now one of the resurgent area's art studios (Testhouse 5).

TEA TIME

Earl Grey liked the flavour of tea flavoured with bergamot so much that he asked Twinings, his local supplier, to produce the doctored brew commercially. His Grace's fad proved massively successful, so it is hardly surprising that the company located its Newcastle factory on Earl Grey Way. The founder of the business, Thomas Twining, had an eye for public figures, 'celebs' as we might now label them. He once let Hogarth paint his portrait to settle a tea bill.

LUCOZADE

Frederick Pybus, a celebrated surgeon practising at the RVI, was responsible for that universal comforter of childhood ailments. Orderlies at the hospital who had worked in First World War field hospitals reported that patients given soft drinks had suffered no ill consequences. This was rather against the grain since perceived wisdom dictated it was better not to prescribe liquids. Pybus experimented with various blends of glucose and fruit flavourings put together by a local pharmacist, W.W. Hunter, working from the Barras Bridge pharmacy of Owen & Son. Originally called 'Glucozade', the product first went on sale in 1927. The name was changed to 'Lucozade' in 1929. This wonderful elixir was snapped up by Thomas Beecham's in 1938, shortly before they added the equally iconic Brylcreem to their expanding range.

Frederick Pybus kept on experimenting. He noted positive results in a diabetic patient treated with human cadaveric pancreatic tissue (yum) and is credited with the idea of pancreatic transplantation. It required a mere forty-two years for the idea to be realised.

KEEP IT CLEAN

Andrews Liver Salts acquired their name from the parish church of St Andrew in the city centre. Mr Scott, who was a lay preacher at the church and his partner in the margarine importing business, came up with a new remedy for indigestion. We don't know if the name came from the church itself or the fact that their offices were located nearby. Indeed, another story suggests that their offices at Andrews House (no. 4 Gallowgate) were named after the product! Presumably, Scott did not need the traditional hangover cure associated with their oft-employed remedy, but you have to wonder about Mr Turner. He and a Mr Phillips went on to develop Milk of Magnesia.

Scott and Turner are further credited with the creation of Delrosa Rosehip Syrup. During the Second World War local children were paid 3*d* per pound to collect rosehips for processing at factories in Wallsend and Newcastle. The inventors' company, at that point branded Phillips, Scott & Turner, duly expanded into Sterling Health.

ON YER BIKE

Tyneside bakers Greggs now own over 1,400 stores spread across the nation. Founding proprietor John Gregg started out by delivering yeast on his bike, so all those grateful Newcastle lasses could bake their own stotties. He went off to war in 1914 leaving another one of the lasses, wife Elsie, in charge. She preferred vans to bikes and started selling confectionery and eggs as well. Clearly a woman with an eye for business; by 1939 they had enough capital to build their own bakery and opened an initial outlet in Gosforth twelve years later.

THE ABOMINABLE TRADE

The UK connection to the pernicious practice of slavery is generally associated with Liverpool, Glasgow, Bristol or Whitehaven, yet the mercantile elite of Newcastle were more involved than might be imagined. Merchant adventurers from the region beginning with the Hylton family in the early seventeenth century established links with the growing plantation culture in the new American colonies and the Caribbean.

Many local families, the Trevelyans of Wallington, Ogles, Fenwicks and Cadogans, acquired sugar plantations. Demand for sugar was insatiable and rising. John Graham Clarke who'd come from East Yorkshire on militia duty, married the wealthy widow Elizabeth Rutter, owner of the town's premier brewery. He prospered mightily in the Atlantic trade, had a hand-span of ships and a dozen and more plantations to his name. His fine house once stood where the fire station now stands on the corner of Pilgrim Street and Worswick Street. Local ironfounders manufactured the shackles used to chain the slaves, the tide of human misery that provided labour to work the plantations.

GEORDIE AT TABLE –
FOOD AND DRINK

I'm a broken-hearted keelman and I'm o'er head in love
With a young lass from Gateshead an I call her me dove.
Her name's Cushie Butterfield and she sells yella clay
And her cousin's a muckman an they call him Tom Gray

She's a big lass, she's a bonny lass an she likes her beer
An I call her Cushie Butterfield an I wish she was here
Cushie Butterfield

'Stotty': Many a lunchtime sarnie still comes in a stotty (aka stottie cake). These are flat (usually about 4cm deep), round (20–30cm) and made from heavy dough – the result of only one kneading. Traditionally, they were made with the vestiges of the bread dough. Once the tins had gone into the oven any leftovers were gathered up and 'stotted' (bounced) off the bottom of the oven. Cooking on the hot floor of the oven probably accounts for the low rising of the cake. There are those who maintain they will 'stott' off the floor if dropped after cooking.

The best and favoured way of eating them is split then filled with ham and pease pudding (another Newcastle treat). Mind you, there are those who swear by bacon, egg and sausage. Fried egg and tomato is pretty cool as well.

BROON!

Newcastle Brown Ale has been a local symbol since 1925 when Colonel J. Porter first came up with the recipe for the Tyne Brewery (one of the Newcastle Breweries group). It went into production in 1927; legends about strength and taste arose almost immediately. It is said local police demanded a reduction in strength within a mere span of 24 hours because the cells had filled up so rapidly! Rumours of a 'Brown Ale' ward at the local addictions clinic were still circulating after brewing moved to Tadcaster in 2010.

It became the defining brew of Scottish & Newcastle after it acquired Newcastle Breweries in 1960. The famous blue star which became their logo was actually taken from the bottle design of 1928; each of the five points represents one of the local breweries which came together to form the Newcastle group. These days it is owned by Heineken who sell it all over the world. They say demand in the United States outstrips supply and that it is one of the best selling beers in China (where Heineken has a plant).

ENTERTAINMENT

Newcastle was presented with 25 per cent of William Wallace after he had been hanged, drawn and quartered in London in 1305. We hung it over a sewer, probably in recognition of the threat posed to the town by one of the numerous raids he'd launched: Newcastle 1, Scots 0.

When did Air Force One land at Newcastle Airport? It was on 6 May 1977 when Jimmy Carter came to say a thank you for our welcoming the 'Friendship Force' set up by his spouse, Rosalyn Carter. People can't help joining in; we all want to be Geordies. Mind, he can't have been that overwhelmed, as he only stayed four hours. And we do tend to eat a lot of peanuts.

The Friendship Force proper stayed a bit longer. An empty Pan Am 747 charter plane named 'Clipper Friendship' was ordered from Brussels to Newcastle to take 381 of them back to Atlanta. At 6.30 a.m. on 4 July 1977 the aircraft departed Newcastle but had to be refuelled in Shannon (Ireland) because the runway of Newcastle airport was too short for a fully loaded Jumbo. The pilot was almost shocked by the answer to his question, 'How many big planes have ever landed at this small airport?' The answer was: 'You're the first!'

It was all the dawn of a beautiful friendship – Jimmy returned in 1987 and Atlanta remains one of Newcastle's twinned cities. The University of Northumbria has subsequently been designated as the 'European Centre of the University System of Georgia' and a memorial stone to the American president stands in the grounds of Newcastle Civic Centre.

We are also twinned with the cities of Bergen in Norway, Gelsenkirchen in Germany, Groningen in Holland, Haifa in Israel, Nancy in France and of course Newcastle in Australia. Not a lot of people know that we have a Friendship Agreement with Little Rock, Arkansas, USA.

Newcastle has a particularly close bond with Norway. King Olav V opened Newcastle's new Civic Centre in 1968 and each December, the city is presented with a Christmas tree by the citizens of Bergen. The custom originated after the Second World War as a symbol of peace and goodwill. Bergen wished to express its gratitude for the role played Tyneside servicemen in liberating their city from the Nazis and there is a plaque inside the Civic Centre commemorating the connection. King Harald, son of King Olav, was also made a freeman of the city on the anniversary of the opening, forty years later. Other freemen of the city include Nelson Mandela, Sir Bobby Robson, and Northern Rock (pre the unfortunate tenure of Adam Applegarth needless to say).

MUMMY, MUMMY

Entertainment takes strange forms; mummy-unwrapping for example. The mummy of Irtyru is now in the Great North Museum at the Hancock. She was found in Egypt by Napoleon Bonaparte's expedition who sent her back to Europe. She made her way to Bath where she was purchased by John Bowes Wright who donated her to the Literary & Philosophical Society of Newcastle upon Tyne – generally referred to as the Lit & Phil.

There, in March 1830, she fell victim to a current craze – public unrolling in, as we are told, the 'presence of a large number of members'. She was the first (and last) unrolling in the region. Just as well really. It took two hours (which suggests reasonable care in an era when the performance had been known to take only thirty minutes).

Three surgeons removed 22.5kg of bandages. Those organs still in the body were sent to the Royal Infirmary for study, never to be seen again.

That was only the beginning. An x-ray taken in the 1960s revealed a metal staple fixing her spine to the coffin back board so that she could be stood up. Just to be sure, the top of her skull had been lifted and a hook to hang her on inserted. Neither can now be removed without damaging the mummy. The varnish used to seal everything trapped mould under her elbow and she also acquired a dose of carpet beetle.

Another mummy, this time Bakt en Hor, took revenge in advance for any potential indignities. Customs officers who hacked off the bottom of the boxed coffin to check that the contents really were as stated were scared witless when they found themselves holding part of a foot. Swiftly patched together she was bundled off to Newcastle where the Lit & Phil put her on display for a few days each week. Members of the public could pay a small amount to pop in for a look but nobody thought to post a watch in the room. Whoever walked off with the still loose baseboard was never found.

Along with many other items from the Lit & Phil's natural history collection, she went off to the Hancock Museum to be displayed with a shawl draped over her from the neck down. This concealed the fact that her head had been mounted on a broom-shank

In recent years, the Hancock Museum underwent extensive renovation and extension, reopening as the Great North Museum at the Hancock. That joy of many a Tyneside childhood, the collection of stuffed animals, went back on display in a new form and continues to delight. Menawhile, the mummies went off on holiday to a new location: the Roman fort at Segedunum in Wallsend. There they encountered a local mystic (taxi driver by day/psychic by night) who failed to gain a reading. Shame really, he might have been able to clarify the location of some of the missing mummy wrappings. Not to worry, they turned up again recently in an envelope tucked into one of the Lit & Phil's volumes, quite a bookmark.

WHAT ANCIENT CULINARY FEAT WAS REPLICATED IN THE HANCOCK MUSEUM?

Brewing Tutankhamun's beer. Curator Gillian Scott managed to produce a bottle or two a few years ago. It took some effort and initial attempts to grind the emmer wheat (which was one of the original ingredients) broke a food processor. Fortunately, the ancient method – using a grindstone – worked a treat.

One of the other joys of the new museum is the presence of the Porphyry Foot which used to be housed in a small, out-of-the-way room in the university. It is part of the Shefton Collection, a fabulous gathering of ancient items from Greece and Italy. One of the pleasures on a wet afternoon was to make your way down winding corridors to what felt like a private museum. Repressing the urge to stroke the big toe of the foot, you could spend hours in there without seeing another soul. The foot, three times life size, is now housed along with the rest of the collection in a special section of the new museum where, damn it, you have to share with the rest of the world.

It is perhaps just as well that only the foot has been discovered so far. Extrapolating up from the remains gives you a statue well over 6 metres high.

MODERN FEATS

The shoe tree at the junction where Heaton Park becomes Jesmond Dene represents a feat of acrobatic competence as well as well as a monument to the foot. Dozens of shoes, some in pairs, others single, hang from the highest branches. Nobody ever admits to putting them there but the collection continues to grow.

MUSICAL APLOMB

Newcastle has long been famous for the range and quality of its music. Ranging from the chamber music of eighteenth-century composer Charles Avison to the slightly more modern musings of Sting, the City has provided accommodation and performance venues to some of the great performers.

Our own Northern Sinfonia long had a home at the City Hall although these days they have moved over the river to the Sage Gateshead while modern music makers made the City's clubs renowned.

Jimmy Hendrix stayed in Newcastle for some time during the late 1960s at the home of his then manager, Chas Chandler. The latter was himself famous as a member of the Animals – numerous fans have described Hendrix busking on the streets of Heaton or playing his guitar in the Club Agogo (where it had been suspended from the ceiling).

The Beatles song 'She Loves You' was partly written in Newcastle when Lennon and McCartney were staying at the Turk's Head Hotel; they were in Newcastle to play at City Hall.

Our tradition of musical development continues – ours is the only university in the world to offer a degree in folk music.

HOPPING ABOUT

Ever wondered why there is no beer tent at the Hoppings? Every June for an entire week, the largest travelling funfair in Europe runs on the Town Moor. Over 28 acres of rides, shows and stalls and every year, anyone who fancies a pint to go with their ride has to walk for a minimum of fifteen minutes to find one. That's because this is a Temperance Fair. Presumably the organisers of the first one held in 1882 hoped to provide a healthy alternative to Race Week (which, in that year, was moved to a new home at Gosforth Park).

Boxing, cockfights, gambling booths and vast imbibing that accompanied racing attracted crowds of thousands. Temperance societies hoped to keep those same people occupied with a programme of sports, music, children's games and races (how about 'artistic skipping'?) and military competitions. In the 1950s Sunday was allocated to political speakers and lectures.

There are two theories about the name: one that it derives from dancing (which used to take place) also referred to as 'hopping'. The other is that it derives from the 'hopping about' done by those who had picked up fleas from animals who accompanied the shows.

The Hoppings have always been vulnerable to vagaries of the north-eastern weather. In 1912, damage to grazing following an undending series of downpours caused the fair to be relegated to Jesmond Dene, in exile there for a few years until returned in 1923. There have been three years when the weather was so bad as to merit an extension to allow showmen to drive a return from the event – 1909, 1912 and 1958. It very nearly happened again in 1997 when mud reached quagmire levels: the repair bill soared to £30,000. Even that could not match 2007 when powerful tractors were needed to extricate show vehicles and repairs rocketed to £50,000.

The opening is always a grand event, usually performed by the Mayor of Newcastle. Only once in the history of the Hoppings has the same mayor carried out the duty twice. In 2004, Cllr Margaret Carter found her year in office extended to allow two elections to be held on the same day.

Attendances at this well-loved event have always been high. There were 150,000 who flocked to the first fair (despite an annoying insistence on accompanying every prize giving with a civic address). Numbers had climbed to nearly a million by the dawn of this present century.

GOING TO THE DOGS

The first dog show in history took place in Newcastle on 28–29 June 1859. It was organised as a publicity stunt by William Rochester Pape (the gunmaker) and John Shorthose (a brewer's agent). Both men had business in mind. Until then, showing animals had been a largely informal affair, conducted in the backyards of pubs.

Pape wanted to connect with a ready audience for his guns, hence the restriction of classes at the show to setters and pointers – gun dogs of the day. Only male exhibitors were allowed (no respectable woman would have anything to do with matches and shows held in pubs anyway) and only male dogs could be shown.

Some questions about the results of this show did arise. The Mayor of Newcastle entered two animals but neither was placed. The winning pointer's owner was Mr W. Jobling of Morpeth (whose brother Mr J. Jobling happened to be one of the judges). The relationship between setter category winner J. Brailsford and setter judge R. Brailsford was never clarified but we may assume one existed. The prize, one of

Mr Pape's admirable guns, was worth £15–£20. Quite an investment given that the show was advertised as running at a loss of £15.

Pape, now famous as the inventor of choke boring, which effectively made breech-loading guns possible, had premises in Collingwood Street and Neville Street. The title 'Pape' can just be made out on the wall of a building opposite the Central station. The gunmaker was an expert in that particularly Victorian invention, the gentle art of PR – he advertised his business as running since 1830 (he was born in 1831). He finally died in 1923 of head injuries suffered when he was knocked down by a delivery truck. His well-established concern was taken over in 1935 by Bagnall & Kirkwood who still run the landmark gun shop in Grey Street, Newcastle.

ANYONE FOR TENNIS?

Muriel Robb, a member of Jesmond Lawn Tennis Club in Newcastle, played in the Wimbledon singles event four times and was never less than a quarter-finalist. In 1902 she won the women's singles championship, PLUS the Irish, Welsh and Scottish national singles titles. No man or woman had achieved this feat before her and none has done so since. In those days before tie-breaks, her singles win was the longest women's final in history in terms of the number of games. She also triumphed in the mixed doubles and three times in the women's doubles. She served overarm at a time when most women favoured underarm, and ranged over the court more widely than the contemporary norm.

She died at her home in Osborne Road in Jesmond at the very early age of twenty-eight and was buried in Jesmond Old Cemetery. It is said that at her funeral the wreaths were so numerous that two lorries were needed to transport them.

MORE FAMOUS VISITORS TO THE CITY

Dara O'Briain: the comedian has publicly declared his acquisition of a chair from a certain Newcastle comedy club. He stated that he sat in it all the way back to London, as there were no other seats left on the train.

Yevgeny Zamyatin: what do you mean, you've never heard of him? He was the first ever Russian science-fiction writer (most famous for his novel *We*). Newcastle had earlier played host to a number of Russian revolutionary types prior to 1917 and a few Soviet spies to be in the years after that.

Zemyatin worked at Armstrong Whitworth in 1916 supervising the building of the world's largest icebreaker, *Svyatogor*, later to be renamed *Krasin*. Famous as the ship which rescued General Umberto Nobile in 1928 when his balloon expedition to the North Pole foundered, she saw extensive service during the Second World War and is now a floating museum. The story of her rescue of the explorer and her team was filmed in 1969 as *The Red Tent* starring Peter Finch, Claudia Cardinale and Sean Connery.

There is a plaque on the site of his home in Jesmond.

THIS IS THE VOICE OF THE MYSTERONS

What is the link between Captain Scarlet and a cartoon of Romans on the netty? Answer: Ron Embleton. Every Geordie child knows them: Frank Graham's books about the Romans complete with cartoons by Ron Embleton. The really famous one is a group of legionaries sharing a latrine . . . they're passing round a sponge on a stick. Then follows that wonderful moment when somebody tells you what they used for toilet paper and all the 'oohs' of disgust go round.

Ron did the pictures of Captain Scarlet that were shown at the end of every episode. He also drew the long running *Penthouse* cartoon, Wicked Wanda.

He and Frank Graham met when the pair of them holidayed in Tunisia. Embleton would go on to produce over 140 paintings of this area and sold six million postcards featuring his scenes of Roman life. The latrine painting alone sold one million cards.

FREE WITH TODAY'S PAPER

Ralph Hedley (1848–1913) was best known for his portrayals of everyday life. His painting, 'Cat in a Cottage Window' is famous worldwide and was painted at his home in Spital Tongues. Hedley was a serious artist, a member of the Royal Society of British Artists and had more than forty paintings displayed at the Royal Academy.

He was also one of the earliest painters to have his work given away by a newspaper. Copies of 'Going Home' were distributed by the *Newcastle Chronicle* in its Christmas 1889 edition. The print, showing a pair of miners on their way home after a shift, was massively popular and found its way onto the walls of thousands of homes in the area. So profound was the impact that the NUM commissioned a statue of the younger miner, George Blyth, to decorate their headquarters building (Burt Hall) in Northumberland Road.

Of course, sometimes you need a sideline to make a living. He founded a monumental sculpture business in St Mary's Place in 1869 subsequently inherited by his sons, Roger and Frederick. The family specialised in religious themes and examples of their work can be found in St Nicholas' Cathedral, St Chads' in Hartlepool and All Saints', Gosforth.

LOCAL PATRONAGE

The famous statue of Earl Grey which gives its name to Monument area was carved by the same sculptor who put Nelson on his column in London – Edward Hughes Bailey. The statue was struck by lightning in 1941, sending his Grace's head flying to the ground where the pieces were retrieved by an enterprising local shopkeeper. He popped it in the window with a sign, 'Our furniture is so good even Earl Grey came down to see it.' A postie driving his van, narrowly missed by the flying stone, may have wished the visit had never taken place.

The head was glued together in 1947 and a plaster cast taken. Roger Hedley (son of Ralph) was responsible for recarving the cranium we see today. An internal circular staircase runs up the inside of the column and is opened to access to a platform below the statue. Mind, you had better be fit, there are 162 steps and very little light!

HALF THE JOB

We are used to seeing the Laing Art Gallery full of magnificent paintings and local artefacts. Indeed, the crowds for the first exhibition in 1904 were so lively the police had to be called to tame them. A Scottish wine & spirit merchant by the name of Alexander Laing offered £20,000 towards building a gallery for the city in which he had made his fortune. That was in 1900. Some things do not change, including the way building costs always overrun. By the time it opened in 1904 it had cost Laing 50 per cent more than he had bargained for. Perhaps that's why he did not offer any money to purchase items to display, just the shell in which to house them.

Wealthy local solicitor Arthur Shipley left his collection of 2,500 fine paintings plus £30,000 in cash to the City of Newcastle when he died in 1909. You'd think this would be the perfect solution. Unfortunately, for some reason, he specifically excluded the Laing from benefiting from this legacy. After much public debate, Newcastle rejected the donation and it went to Gateshead where Mr Shipley had been born. They built a gallery especially for it.

THE FIRST ART EXHIBITION IN TOWN

This was organised by Thomas Miles Richardson in 1822 from his studio in Blackett Street. In fact, he organised a whole series of them from 1822 to 1845. Richardson, his six sons and his nephew dominated the Newcastle art scene in the early part of the nineteenth century. He painted some very familiar views of the city – Grainger Street, for example – as well as locations on Tyneside and in Northumberland.

These were not shows as we think of them in a strictly cultural context. They were intended as sales opportunities; the only pictures on show were those by Richardson and his inner circle – quarrel with him and you were out!

VIZ A VIZ

Now a part of Newcastle history, *Viz* it has even had its own exhibition in the Lit & Phil. It was called *Viz* for a very practical reason: the letters are the easiest ones to carve out of cork tiles. That's because the first issues were carved using a printing set made from tiles belonging to Chris Donald's father. It's full of local life such as Parkie the park keeper who is supposed to be based on one who used to yell at Chris Donald as he walked home from school across Jesmond Dene. Roger Mellie could apparently be seen in the old Tyne Tees TV days when various presenters drank in a pub across the road from the studios.

LOCAL WRITING

Where do you start? There are dozens of them! Chaz Benchley, Jack Higgins, Carol Clewlow, Jack Common, Basil Bunting, Ian la Frenais, etc. Then there are the ones who simply lived here for a while like Joseph Conrad. There are those who use the city as a setting, too, including Martin Waites, Peter Flannery and Catherine Cookson.

ACTING UP

Jimmy Nail, Bill Travers, Greg Wise, Janet McTeer, Tod Slaughter, Denise Welsh – keep going . . . Newcastle has a tradition of giving young and developing thespians a chance to acquire their skills. Live Theatre was founded in 1973 by, among others, Tim Healy and has helped launch the careers of actors like Robson Green. For much of that time it has been based on the Quayside. The building's career mirrors changes in the area, transforming from a run-down post-industrial site to one of the most stylish and interesting venues in the area.

The Peoples Theatre in the east end of the city has been around for even longer. It started in 1911 as a fundraising sub-committee of the British Socialist Party. An early participant was Colin Veitch, captain of Newcastle United FC and organiser of one of the first footballers' strikes. By 1914 war had broken out, and not just in France. The party felt the drama group were not serious enough, that the party was, 'violently opposed to the Socialist Faith being stained, sullied and contaminated by the now pernicious connection.'

Nonetheless, the drama group went from strength to strength, performing a range of new radical drama and attracting attention and support from national figures like George Bernard Shaw. They moved to premises in Leazes Park Road, then to Rye Hill and finally to the current site in Heaton. Peggy Ashcroft and John Gielgud were supporters of the building fund established to achieve the final move. Over the years a number of well-known actors and performers have been given their initial grounding at the Peoples including Jack Shepherd, Kevin Whately, Neil Tennant, Ross Noble and Angela Riseborough.

Live Theatre, the quayside revitalised as a centre for culture.

There were over sixty-five theatres and cinemas in Newcastle at one point, most now gone. The Grand Theatre in Byker hosted repertory companies which included such luminaries as Kenneth More while Theatre Royal in the city centre has had numerous visits from famous names as well as hosting annual tours by the RSC.

WHICH ITALIAN SOAP FEATURED A GEORDIE LASS?

The hugely popular long-running programme *Un Medico in Famiglia* featured Newcastle-born Shivani Ghai. An inability to speak Italian proved no barrier and her performances were acclaimed. She'd come to their attention through her roles in a number of British shows such as *Spooks* and a performance as the bride in *Bride and Prejudice*. She went on to appear in *The House of Saddam*. Her film *Cleanskin*, also featuring Sean Bean was released in 2011.

MORE FILMED IN NEWCASTLE

Women in Love? Well, nearly. Glenda Jackson goes into a bar at one point: the Central is in Gateshead, just over the river. All she had to do was keep on walking and she would have been over the Tyne Bridge. Ken Russell liked filming up here; one of his early documentaries was about Bedlington Pit. He used the same location in this film (although he had to get the machinery put back since the pit had closed in the meantime).

Stormy Monday features a jazz band parade – no, not a parade with jazz players in it – a 'jazz band'. These were a north-east phenomenon from the 1950s through to the 1980s, usually based in mining communities. Large groups of mostly juvenile girls, dressed as American-style cheerleaders, would parade through the streets playing kazoos, drums and the odd glockenspiel. They performed stock favourites like 'When the Saints Go Marching In' and were seriously competitive. The Pelaw Hussars feature in one of the most famous scenes in *Get Carter*.

MOVEABLE ART

Newcastle has over 100 pieces of public art ranging from the Dragon Gate at the entrance to Chinatown to the statue of Queen Victoria in front of the hospital that bears her name.

Pinning them down can be a hard business. Do you remember Vulcan – seven metres tall – a bronze monumental sculpture by Paolozzi which stood in Central Square for nine years? The statue of the Greek god of the forge was a reference to Tyneside's industrial past, exploring the theme of man and robot. Then one day it turned into a spiral decorated with shopping trolleys because Vulcan went off on his travels – to Gloucester Cathedral to take part in a year-long exhibition there. The good news is he's due back.

Let's hope we get to keep the replacement which was commissioned by the Somerfield supermarket group. The double helix of shopping trolleys by Abigail Fallis was unveiled by James Watson, one of the joint discoverers of the DNA configuration. It raises all sorts of questions about the make up of modern society and is the first in a series of temporary works of art that will make use of this site.

'Wor Jackie' is a statue of celebrated footballer Jackie Milburn by Susannah Robinson. Jackie Milburn is a legendary figure in the north-east and is still widely loved by Newcastle fans. He joined the team in 1943 and remained in the area after his retirement, working as the north-east football correspondent for the *News of the World* for over twenty years. His prowess in and flair for the game are indisputable – he

('Wor') Jackie Milburn, the famous Newcastle United footballer and one of the area's favourite sons.

scored 283 goals in 492 appearances. Seems to have been a family habit, his nephews Jack and Bobby Charlton were pretty good too.

The statue, which shows Milburn kicking a ball, began life on Northumberland Street in 1995, at which point the ball started rolling – literally. It has been stolen at least three times, usually to be recovered from nearby. On the final occasion, in 1996, it was completely removed but was eventually discovered in Jesmond Dene. The whole effort was moved to St James Boulevard, close to the football ground. A good place for him – another larger statue by Tom Maley was nearby. Nobody has seen the latter for a while though, which does raise the odd question – how do you lose an 8ft bronze statue? If anyone knows where it got to . . .

Then there was 'Man with Pigeons', a near life-size statue of a pigeon fancier surrounded by his flock that in 1976 was stood in Old Eldon Square by developers of that new shopping centre of the same name. The sculptor, André Wallace, is also responsible for the River God statue (1996) down on the Quayside. 'Man with Pigeons' has had a chequered career, moving a number of times before finally settling down beside one of the escalators inside the building. One of his pigeons has been lifted a few times as well but always seems to return, a homing bird perhaps? Or are rumours of spare pigeons kept in a council warehouse perhaps true? This was certainly the case for the replacement footballs used to replenish the Jackie Milburn statue, mentioned above!

MAGIC CARPETS

And then there is the 'Blue Carpet' which has not moved much, although there are those who think the colour has. This public square has been paved in tiles created from glass shards set in resin and designed to look like a real carpet curving up around seating and bollards. What was intended to be an intense blue, strikes this author, like many, as a rather washed-out grey. The artist apparently experienced some difficulty in getting the right shade of blue from manufacturers which provided some entertainment as tile after tile of what looked like the same shade was laid out in rows in the Civic Centre.

The carpet cost £1.4 million (more than five times the original budget) and took six years to complete. What it did achieve was an intense amount of public debate in local papers. Presumably the strength of feeling accounts for an attempt to set fire to it shortly before work was completed which cost an additional £10,000 to repair; 100 of the 22,500 tiles were damaged.

A £36,000 refit was necessary within five years of installation, at which point an opportunity was taken to replace the lighting system underneath, hopefully saving hard-pressed council tax payers some £60,000 over the ensuing decade.

CAST IN CONCRETE

Public reaction to the square is nothing compared to the views expressed about the 'concrete men' (now thankfully deceased). Officially this art work/safety barrier around Haymarket Metro station was entitled 'Shoulder to Shoulder' although locals rapidly took to calling them Lego Men. A local councillor, who was at the original planning meeting, had an interesting insight to offer on the process. He described the first design as looking like the gender signs on a public toilet and claimed to be only marginally surprised when the next set of plans incorporated a fountain which bore striking resemblance to a urinal!

This work attracted widespread criticism, especially from members of the public who got soaked when the sprays malfunctioned in high winds. Eventually they had to be turned off and suggestions about what to do with the structure began to emerge. One councillor attracted some measure of public support by suggesting that any one willing to bear the costs of removal should be given them for free. After ten years they were finally taken into storage pending redevelopment of the site and were last seen lying in a field in the east end of the city.

RATHER BETTER EFFORTS

But enough – what about those that really do work and there are many. Take Nicolaus Widerberg's figures adorning the outside of the Baring

Gallery at Northumbria University and the walkway commissioned to link City campus with the new site over the motorway. Deceptively simple, bronze 'Pillar Man' marks the course of one of Newcastle's underground streams while the granite figures on the walkway satisfy mind and senses. They even satisfy curiosity, each one has the artist's initials hidden somewhere about it; you can while away plenty of time trying to track them down.

Or take 'Man with Potential Selves' at the end of Grainger Street. The three bronze figures are actually 2.5 metres tall, even though they give the appearance of being real human beings (albeit doing strange things, like floating sideways in space with no support). Impossible to ignore, they have become hugely popular, especially with very drunk youngsters who flood past them in search of a taxi on a Friday night. Offerings of food, cans of beer, even newspapers get pressed into their hands. The one whose foot lifts slightly off the ground can often be found grinding out a cigarette under his heel. And some of us who left their glasses at home can be found addressing the figures in passing.

DIALECT

Gan canny where yer gannin
With new skeets upon yer feet
Cos the tiket mans a cumin
Tappy lappy doon the street
Aan aah can't afford te pay him
This week he's getting not
Cos the scullery flair wants diyin
Aah've te buy the tarry toot
Se divvint scuff yer new skeets
Cos they'll have te gan te hock
Unless there's oot agannin
Doon alang the dock
So gan canny where yer gannin
Mind yer Ps and Qs
And what ivvor ye are diyin
Tek care them bloody shoes
'Geordie's New Shoes' by Irv Graham

Whether 'Geordie' derives from local artisans acclaiming George I during the 1715 Jacobite Rebellion or whether inspired by George Stephenson's design for a safety lamp, the dialect is a direct descendant from the speech of those first Anglian warriors. Proof if any were needed is that Bede's works translate more fluently into Geordie than modern English. What constitutes the precise geographical spread of Geordie dialect is more contentious, some perceive the term being restricted to Newcastle upon Tyne only, others see a spread through the region. Nobody local would confuse Geordie with Mackem although the *Oxford English Dictionary* refuses to countenance any date for the latter before 1988!

Nae agreement about wor Geordie:

'Geordie', according to the *Oxford English Dictionary*, has been used since 1876 to describe miners. The name may well be connected to the preference in this area for George Stephenson's miners safety lamp.

Another explanation also involves Stephenson. He was a bit on the forthright side: 'his blunt speech and dialect drew contemptuous sneers' from a Parliamentary commission he had been summoned to address. It was not long before keelmen were allowed to share the name as they were viewed as sharing similar characteristics.

Local impresario Billy Purvis was said to have hurled the phrase at a rival in 1823. Legend has it was intended as a reference to poor mad George III

7

MINISTERS, RANTERS & WITCHES

BEGINNINGS

During the Anglo-Saxon period Northumbria enjoyed its 'Golden Age', an era of prosperous monasticism ushered in by Wilfrid's triumph over far less worldly Celtic monks at the Synod of Whitby in 664. Bede brought this age of glorious creative achievement to its sublime pinnacle but successive Viking raids and the inexorable decline of the Northern Kingdom led to collapse and decay. It was not until some eight years after Hastings that Aldwin, a Gloucestershire monk with two fellows from the monastery at Evesham, arrived after a long and no doubt perilous journey on foot. They found their destination, Tynemouth Abbey, largely ruined and took up residence at Jarrow. This marked the beginning of a post-Conquest monastic revival.

By 1082, a community had been re-established on Lindisfarne, another at Tynemouth, with Augustinians at Hexham and Brinkburn, Cistercians at Newminster (Morpeth) and Premonstratensians at both Alnwick and Blanchland. Nunneries sprang up at Holystone in Coquetdale and at Guyzance; a rash of churches were restored and extended. This great burst of renaissance activity was funded largely by cash or land grants from feudal magnates and gentry. A great many of those who chose to enter holy orders were themselves men and woman of rank and position; this was part of a process of 'Normanisation', now that the Scots' attempt to extend their own frontier southwards had been seen off. The Battle of the Standard effectively marked the end of Alba's dreams.

'TWO KINGS IN ENGLAND'

Key 'players' in this new regional establishment were the Prince Bishops of Durham, none more regal than Anthony Bek who held office from 1284 to 1311. His steward wrote: 'There are two kings in England, namely the Lord King of England, wearing a crown as a sign of his regality and the Lord Bishop of Durham, wearing a mitre in place of a crown, in sign of his regality in the Diocese of Durham.' In the Anglian kingdom, Bishops of Durham had represented natural successors to the Bishops of Lindisfarne. Even during the hegemony of the Wessex kings these northern earls and bishops had retained a very considerable degree of autonomy.

William the Conqueror first attempted to maintain the status quo but, faced with open rebellion and the destruction at Durham of Robert de Commines with his followers, he reverted to less diplomatic means – the notorious 'Harrying of the North'. The last Anglo-Saxon Bishop of Durham expired in prison and the vacant see devolved upon William Walcher of Lorraine. After the current earl, Waltheof, perished beneath the headsman's axe, King William merged the two appointments and elevated Walcher to 'Earl Bishop'. One of this magnate's primary responsibilities was to secure the northern frontier against further Scottish expansion or inroads, potent threats during this era. Walcher enjoyed no more popularity than his immediate predecessors and was murdered at Gateshead in 1081.

LAND OF THE PRINCE BISHOPS

Undeterred, William Rufus, upon succeeding his fearsome parent, appointed Bishop William St Carileph, though his temporal writ ran only south of the Tyne and Derwent bringing into existence the County Palatine of Durham – Land of the Prince Bishops – while Northumberland became a wholly separate county. The Prince Bishops exercised considerable sway in Durham, England's northern bastion, retaining extensive estates and considerable influence within the wild frontier zone of Northumberland. Their autonomous powers, jealously guarded, were considerable. They could raise a regional parliament – echoes of which we've seen recently in the abortive 'Regional Assembly'. The Prince Bishops could and did raise forces for the defence of the north, they maintained independent jurisdiction, levied taxes and customs dues, appointed sheriffs, granted charters and established fairs and markets.

BEK

Perhaps none of the Prince Bishops better exemplified their quasi-regal independence than Anthony Bek. Son of a gentry family and educated at Oxford, Bek (born *c.* 1245) was in his forties when he ascended to his see. He had earlier accompanied Edward I ('Longshanks') on crusade and occupied important lay positions within the Royal Household. He remained a trusted advisor to the king and campaigned actively during the early musters of the Anglo-Scottish wars, leading the vanguard at the battle of Falkirk in 1298.

As a result of a simmering and fractious feud with Richard de Hoton, Prior of Durham, Bek fell foul of his choleric monarch and was twice dispossessed. It required the intervention of Pope Clement V to secure his position when he was further awarded the additional and highly prestigious office of Patriarch of Jerusalem. The Prince Bishop enjoyed a less volatile relationship with the sybaritic Edward II who restored all of his rights and privileges. In the last years of his active career, Bek was regarded as the senior clerical figure in England and elder statesman; he even reconciled his differences with the priory!

CHURCHES

In Newcastle, St Nicholas', latterly the cathedral, began as chief parish church; one of four built within the ring of medieval walls. The others were All Saints' (extensively rebuilt by the architect David Stephenson between 1786 and 1796), St Andrew's and St John's. An expanding population during the eighteenth century inspired the building of St Ann's Church in 1768 off City Road. This 'stately classical church' replaced an earlier medieval chapel and continues to lend an air of elegance to rather pedestrian surroundings.

Twice as many religious houses were also to be found, these represented a material shift away from the earlier, more worldly foundations in the shire. Present day Nun Street commemorates the former Benedictine

Nunnery of St Bartholomew's (founded in 1135). Grey Friars, on Pilgrim Street (1237), housed the Franciscans, and a fragment of the Austin Friars House (1291) survives in the precincts of the Holy Jesus Hospital. On what are presently Forth and Orchard Streets the Carmelites, or White Friars, were established by 1262 and Black Friars, the Dominican house (*c.* 1250), existed on the southern flank of what is now Stowell Street. Much of this remains and has been carefully conserved. Originally endowed by Sir Peter Scott, a wealthy merchant, this and the other urban or mendicant orders depended to a significant extent upon external patronage and largesse to provide income.

The Dominican house extended over a 7-acre site, possessing both gardens and four small closes, which would contribute to running costs. The house was held on trust as the friars were not, under the rules of their order, permitted to own property outright. The much-decayed buildings were acquired by Newcastle Corporation in the middle of the last century, being finally and extensively restored in the late 1970s. At one point there seemed a possibility the Dominicans might return but the preserved remains now house a series of craft workshops and restaurant. Blackfriars is an ocean of historic tranquillity just within the walls at their most intact, surrounded now by the bustle and glitz of the city's Chinatown district.

A TALE OF TWO CATHEDRALS

St Nicholas' became the cathedral church following a grant of civic status in 1882 – in the same year the Newcastle Diocese was established, carved from the ancient fief of the Prince Bishops. In many ways St Nicholas' retains the character of a medieval parish church, less grand than such lofty establishments as Durham and York. The lantern tower is a marked feature and led Grey in his *Chorographia* of 1649 to exclaim that it 'lifteth up a head of majesty high above the rest, as a cypress tree above the low shrubs.'

Newcastle may also boast of a second cathedral, the Roman Catholic St Mary's, located on Clayton Street West. This is a very fine building designed by the great A.W.N. Pugin in the mid-nineteenth century. In fact the present spire was not part of Pugin's original vision, being completed by his successors Dunn & Hansom in 1872. Local

architects Napper Collerton were responsible for extensive and most careful restoration during the 1980s. Pevsner comments that a Pugin exterior is likely more ornate than his interiors and so it is but the lofty rise of the nave is very pleasing, both confident and airy. The great architectural historian and writer concludes the main church and additions 'forms a most successful group, varied, yet not with any levity.'

REFORMERS AND RECUSANTS

When Henry VIII, from 1536, embarked upon the wholesale dismantling of the existing religious life of the community, the single nunnery and all five Newcastle friaries were wound up and all that valuable land they covered sold on, either to burgesses or speculators. By this time, the institutions had declined remarkably with only three score incumbents between the lot. Blackfriars was perhaps, in the historical context, the most fortunate in that the corporation leased the site to a consortium of guilds. During subsequent centuries, these lay users carried out a host of alterations and continued in sporadic occupation until well into the nineteenth century. As meetings were held on a quarterly basis, the property was used for a host of different purposes, not uncommonly as grace and favour dwellings.

In the surrounding shire and its remoter extremities, distance from London meant local priests were removed from effective central control and were perhaps more recusant in their practices than would otherwise have been the case. The wild reaches of North Tynedale were truly distant from the Episcopal seat of Durham and local gentry, names resonating from the dark days of the steel bonnets, exercised more control than any bishop. Allied to a certain innate and xenophobic conservatism were a cadre of poorly educated clergy serving very large parishes (Newcastle had only four) and who were often subject to rumours of incompetence or poor behaviour.

At the same time as the mercantile elite were becoming versed in new ideas radiating outwards from the capital, easy access to the ports and the frequent comings and goings from the Continent made a convenient staging post for Catholic priests, nuns, books and tracts – particularly those heading for the homes of recusant families such as the Howards, Widdringtons and their affinities. Social and family connections protected many of these families and would lead the Parliamentarians and Scots alike to complain of the *malignant* (Popish) nature of the city and the Earl of Newcastle's army. Nonetheless, there was clearly a strong anti-Catholic element within the corporation. In 1630 Zacharias van der Steen of Liège complained he had been imprisoned in the town gaol for three years because the French ship which had given him passage was suspected of transporting priests! This was not an isolated incident.

DAMNED PURITANS

From the beginning of the seventeenth century there are traces of puritan lecturers in the town associated with the churches of St Nicholas and All Saints'. Activity seems to have been largely individual – transient preachers coming and then going without establishing any significant following – until the arrival of Dr Robert Jennison in the 1630s. It is then that a significant puritan opposition may be seen to arise. His family was both local and well connected – his father and uncle had been mayors. Dissent focussed initially on resisting what were viewed as the Arminianist policies of Durham.

Jennison was opposed to what he regarded as 'popish innovations' – this, among other accusations, led him into conflict with the corporation. In alliance with local merchants such as Dawson,

Maddison and Blakiston, he helped form a significant dissenting faction, based on social, family and trading networks. For example, the puritan mayor, Robert Bewick's eldest son was married to Maddison's sister; Maddison himself had been Mayor in 1632. Sir John Marley complained that Maddison 'was one of the greatest favourers of those of faction in all Newcastle but he carries it warily.'

Connections between Newcastle Puritans and Scots Covenanters led to investigation and repression, particularly as disputes over the role of the bishops escalated. The dissenters were able to force through the election of a puritan mayor in open defiance of the king who was then left with no option but to invite him to London. The inevitable backlash forced the two most notable preachers to flee northwards in 1639/40. The Scots' occupation of the city seemed likely to offer a replacement to the missing leadership but matters moved against the puritans almost immediately. The Scots, of course, were far from welcome; they were an ancient and detested foe. Association with them, even by proxy, condemned those citizens who might, on religious grounds, have welcomed them, 'The common soldiers are intolerably insolent and violent in their actions.' Far from reinforcing the position of the radical religious element, occupation started to turn their fellow citizens against them.

ALTOGETHER A GRAVE SITUATION

> Or should I long, in sorrow's chillness,
> To muse among the silent dead
> Thy cemetery's mural stillness
> Shall tempt my soft and pensive tread.
> *'Jesmond, a Poem' by James Horsley*

Traditionally, townsfolk in Newcastle and other urban settlements were buried in their parish churchyards; indeed they had an established right. As populations swelled, these older graveyards became crowded with fresh arrivals, interments developing in succeeding layers with all the attendant risks of disease and pollution. A couple of gravediggers in Aldgate cemetery in London died from infections in 1832 and a cholera epidemic during the 1850s finally led to the closure of Newcastle's churchyards. For some decades the appeal of out-of-town, suburban cemeteries with abundant space, suitable calm and secured against pernicious 'resurrectionists', had been growing.

In this progressive movement Newcastle proved something of a market leader. Westgate Hill Cemetery was opened in 1829 on a multi-denominational basis 'to the whole human family without difference or distinction.' Seven years later, Newcastle General Cemetery was created. This fashion was soon to be usurped by an even more civic-minded response to the problem. Henry Bell, mayor in 1833, summoned luminaries such as Dobson and Grainger to produce ideas aiming 'to form and establish, for the use of the town, a General Cemetery a measure for which the crowded state of the church yards had long rendered necessary.'

A BETTER CLASS OF BURIAL

A private company was formed with paid-up share capital of £8,000 and the chosen site covered some 11 acres owned by the corporation located in Jesmond, on what was then open ground. In keeping with the prevailing egalitarian spirit, roughly half the space would be consecrated and under the aegis of the parish priest of St Andrew's with the remaining plots reserved for non-conformists.

The prospectus, sent out to shareholders or potential shareholders, stressed that sales of vaults and catacombs would ensure a healthy return – after all, death is an assured market. Dobson began work on the triangular site in 1835, throwing up stout 3-metre high walls and constructing a fine entrance facing what is now Jesmond Road. Two chapels, the Anglican lying on the west and dissenter to the east, were built in fine ashlar. On the southern flank another impressive portal faced out towards Sandyford Road. On 11 November 1836, the Bishop of Durham consecrated the Anglican section and, five days thereafter, the first interment took place.

This was a new age of burials and though young Margaret Hoy, aged only fourteen, from a non-conformist family, was the first to be interred, dissenter vaults did not sell as well as hoped so this section was subsequently annexed and consecrated. Jesmond Cemetery continued in regular use for the next century and more as the expanding suburb grew around, until it survived as an anachronistic Gothic monument in flowing suburban sprawl, with busy roads running along both long sides of the triangle. It survived Hitler but not post-war town planning when, in the iconoclastic 1960s, it was proposed to develop Jesmond Road, by then a commuter bottleneck, into dual carriageway.

This homage to internal combustion would necessitate moving a significant number of burials (over 1,000) and the relocation of the magnificent Dobson entrance. Economic considerations threatened the fact of their survival at all. Effective opposition from residents and conservationists, strengthened by ministerial intervention, saved the day and, though a number of graves were shifted, the entire highway scheme finally collapsed and the cemetery survives. Over 25,000 citizens have been interred there since 1836.

Now the place, which has been partially vandalised in the cause of 'health and safety', one of the more active curses to affect our effete and litigation-obsessed society, still evinces an air of deep and abiding mystery. Largely overgrown with creeper and bushes, a riot of shrouded monuments rise, as though from a Bram Stoker novel. Their almost infinite variety, half-hidden pathways and decaying stonework offer a window to the world of Victorian mortality and funerary practice – many are minor gothic masterpieces in themselves.

SOME NOTABLES

One of those whose mortal remains rest forever in the NW Cemetery is William Campbell (1856–78) who, in life, rejoiced in the unfortunate title of 'heaviest man in Britain'. He died aged only twenty-two but weighing in at 53 stones (with a 96in chest), and was the landlord of the Duke of Wellington public house in High Bridge. Just getting his colossal cadaver out from the third storey on the narrow street proved to require work of engineering ingenuity; exterior brickwork had to be removed and a special hoist installed. In death, the landlord proved as popular as in life, perhaps more so as some 40,000 people attended his cortège, preceded by a full brass band! Near him lies Sid Chaplin (1916–86), the renowned local novelist.

Alexander Laing (1828–1905), the successful wine merchant who endowed the gallery that bears his name, and the pottery manufacturer Christopher Thompson Maling (1824–1901) lie in the same quadrant. John Peter Parland (1801–71) served as a Captain in the Russian Imperial Guard, and his tomb lies near to those of both Archibald Reed (1766–1842), who enjoyed no less than six terms of office as Mayor of Newcastle, and the celebrated artist Thomas Miles Richardson (1784–1848). Moving to the south-west quadrant we find the well-known nineteenth century brewer Robert Deuchar (1831–1904), and laid in the cemetery he designed in the city he transformed is John Dobson (1787–1865). Mark Frater, victim of the Blackett Street murder (see chapter one) lies not far from the two Hancock brothers Albany (1806–73) and John (1808–90), distinguished naturalists both, whose legacy – the venerable Hancock – is now refurbished and extended as the Great North Museum.

Shipbuilders, solicitors (in abundance), booksellers, entrepreneurs – a veritable who's who of industrial age Newcastle crowd Jesmond Cemetery. Here lie William Routland Wilkinson (1819–1902), inventor of reinforced concrete, and Runciman the ship-owner, philanthropist and MP whose grandiose, soaring monument is one of the crowning joys. In the eastern cemetery we find Emerson Bainbridge (1817–1992), stalwart chapelgoer and master draper whose retail consortium remains one of the region's great success stories. Collingwood Bruce, the antiquarian, and Thomas Burt, former pitman who made it into Parliament, rest alongside that other great storekeeper and entrepreneur, John James Fenwick (1846–1905). Dr Newton, surgeon and social reformer; Palliotti, another medical practitioner and Italian Vice-Consul; Andrew Reid the printer; Pumphrey the coffee dealer; Robson the poet; Sutherland the ship-owner and Robert Spence Watson, solicitor, all rest in this quiet and neglected corner.

WITCHES AND WITCH-HUNTERS

Undoubtedly the most notorious of the seventeenth-century witch-hunters was Matthew Hopkins (brought so memorably to life on screen by Vincent Price), self appointed Witchfinder-General whose career of legalised murder blossomed during the uncertainties and breakdown of due process during the Civil Wars. Plague claimed many lives in Newcastle during 1636; a decade later the city, still wasted by the effects of war, was 'visited' again. So desperate were the city fathers that, while rational men all, they were willing to bring out of Scotland the 'Lee Penny'. Legend averred that water was instantly purified once the talisman had been dipped into it. This protection was guaranteed to last for the consumer's lifetime. Needless to say the Penny was available only on a commercial basis.

The Lee family were able to support their product with a host of testimonials and, so impressed and so fanciful was the corporation, they offered to purchase and for a very substantial sum. Fearful of losing their monopoly, the canny owners withdrew their goods and Newcastle was left to its fate. It has been observed that there is considerable and somewhat bitter irony in the fact these same worthies were prepared to condemn others for necromancy – 'Thou shalt not suffer a witch to live' (Exodus XXII v. 18).

This dire vogue for the seeking out and execution of witches reached its dreadful apogee in the mid-seventeenth century when having the witch-finders tour your streets became as ostensibly normal as the midden men.

THE SCOTTISH WITCHFINDER

Citizens were encouraged to denounce their fellow inhabitants, a bit like catching benefit fraudsters today. Any ancient grudge, any intemperate quarrel or hard words could form a handy foundation for an allegation. Those accused were arrested and sent for 'examination' – stripped and manhandled, ostensibly to locate the 'devil's mark' or brand. An awl was used to prick the suspected area of flesh which, if it did not bleed, was certain proof of the diabolical. In this, the examiner had something of a vested interest as each victim condemned brought a bounty of 20s. Newcastle's burgesses turned to Scotland when they felt they required professional assistance in rooting out the local covens. Some writers have insisted that the individual thereby engaged was noted Scottish witch-hunter Jack Kincaid but this is not correct, the practitioner sought by the corporation remains anonymous.

Witchfinders were prone to use awls with retractable blades which would obviously leave no mark. Happily, Lieutenant Hobson, acting as deputy-governor, became suspicious when one of the accused was known to him. Very often those who were accused were lone spinsters and widows, often the most vulnerable and ill-equipped to resist. Hobson did not believe the woman was guilty and on attending the alleged 'examination' immediately suspected trickery when the awl, damningly, did not draw blood. He grabbed the tool from the inquisitor's grasp and jabbed his victim more forcibly, instant bleeding ensued.

Despite this blatant fraud, trials continued and fifteen hapless women were hanged on 21 August 1650, their deathly agonies and limp corpses doubtless providing ample titillation for a hefty crowd on Town Moor. Once the audience had enjoyed their spectacle, the bodies were flung into hasty interment within St Andrew's churchyard. As a final indignity, iron rivets were fastened into the knees of the dead to prevent their rising. Very possibly, any number of other unfortunates died terribly in similar circumstances but the Scot was obliged to quit the city and seek fresh pickings in the county areas. Here, at least, one of the gentry was prepared to take action and the dangerous fraudster fled back into Scotland. Even here, the sanctum of witchfinding provided no further commissions and, with suitable irony, this unknown tormentor was himself accused, condemned and burned Whoever he may have been, he may have been responsible for the judicial murders of some 220 unfortunate women.

THE LAST CAVALIER

One survivor of the city's ancient ramparts is the Sallyport Tower, on the rising ground above Pandon district. This section of the walls, as we have seen, took a fair degree of punishment during the Siege and Storm of 1644. Latterly, the tower, now much altered, became a meeting house for the Carpenter's Guild. Elegant Georgian sashes and a pitched, slated roof replaced the narrow casements and embattled fighting platform. It was said, however, that one last and startling echo of the Civil Wars remained – a ghostly cavalier.

The shade of this long dead incumbent was testified by several generations of caretakers who found his presence more congenial than disturbing. Another witness experienced a spectral vision of the Royalist rising from the floor in a revolving or spiral fashion and then pass through the roof of the chamber – in fact an earlier spiral stair had occupied just this precise location! Disappointingly, the shade of the vanished cavalier has not been sighted in recent decades – perhaps the aged warrior was at last satisfied that the Scots would not return and could quit his final post with honour.

MONKISH PHANTOMS

St Andrew's churchyard has had a distinguished and varied history of interments – no spectral happenings have been recorded although one eighteenth-century sexton appears to have received such a terrible shock while digging a grave that he tumbled lifeless into the excavation! It was rumoured in the late medieval period, prior to the Henrician Dissolution, that relations between incumbents of Blackfriars and their female counterparts within St Bartholomew's Covent (located on the site now occupied by the Grainger Market) were a deal more cordial than religious orders would otherwise advertise. Legend asserts that at least one nun became pregnant after enjoying the embraces of one of her ecclesiastical brethren and was walled in alive for her sin. In consequence, the shadow of her disgraced lover, whose temporal fate in unknown, is said to wander Blackfriars in the dark of late evening and night.

THE TAMBOURINE TAVERN

Towards the western end of St Anne's Street there once stood a rather insalubrious tavern and bawdy house known as the Tambourine. The place had a fairly dark reputation, not just for loose morals and low company but as a place of deep debauchery laced with Satanism. The *Sun* may not have been around at the time but citizens were ever avid for dark tales of degeneracy and necromancy. It was rumoured that a Sandgate Coven met within the bar and their AGM took the form of an *Esbat* where their combined energies would swell to summon the Prince of Darkness himself, presumably as a form of honorary chair for the evening. Imagine the members' ecstasy when, their whispered incantations rising, the Devil duly appeared, though he apparently walked through the door like any mere mortal and showed more interest in the food laid out than diabolical proceedings – the old devil!

Sandgate possessed a fairly unsavoury reputation generally at this time, where hardy keelmen were fleeced of their cash by rapacious landlords and a fluttering of soiled doves whose haunt was there or the Quayside. Keelmen had a reputation for hard drinking. The much harassed wife of one, exasperated by her man's constant insobriety, decided to harness the sinister local connotations to her advantage.

As her husband stayed deaf to her entreaties, she persuaded her brother to deck himself out in a devil outfit and be prepared to leap out and accost her man as he stumbled, legless, from the foetid confines of the Tambourine bar. Her sibling obliged and performed his part most ingeniously, springing out with a suitably demonic flourish; 'Whe are ye' demanded the befuddled husband? 'Ahm the Divil' came the reply, 'an if ye divvent mend yer ways, aal tek ye back wi' me.' 'Whey,' replied the keelman in utter amazement, 'the Divil eh? Ee whey fancy that. Shek me hand 'cause ahm married ter yer sistor!'

MORE GHOSTS

If ye want to rob the deed,
Gan to Jack the Beadle;
He's the man tat steals the leed,
Pop goes the weasel.

In 1858 the city was scandalised by revelations that the Beadle of All Saints', otherwise a bastion of Victorian respectability, had been recycling lead from coffins to line his own purse. This transgression earned him eighteen months' hard labour. Some would say his earthbound spirit still wanders the churchyard in darkness, in penance for his earthly betrayal of trust. Jane 'Jin' Jameson, who we encountered earlier and whose career of debauchery and matricide ended on the gallows, may still haunt her old stamping ground, offering 'fine chence oranges, four for a penny, cherry ripe cornberries, take them and try' entreating late night revellers to seek out her boyfriend, Billy Ellison.

MARTHA WILSON

Nearly forty years before Jack the Beadle's crimes were uncovered a young woman named Martha Wilson hanged herself in a Trinity House Almshouse. Little more is known of her other than, as a suicide, she was denied interment on hallowed ground. From then on her wraith, or 'silky' (the folk name for a female spectre who draws attention to her presence through the subtle movement of her silken attire), became a feature of the Quayside. One of her manifestations was to yet another inebriate keelman (a hard-drinking lot by any standards), who as he staggered rather uncertainly along the Quayside noted a woman across the way keeping pace.

Despite his condition he was aware of something other-worldly about this silent figure and when she turned of up Trinity Chare he, after some hesitation, followed. She stopped, half seen in the gloom ahead, then turned, still without a sound and beckoned him forward. With a return to at least a version of sobriety but still brimful with boldness, he cautiously approached. As she raised her veil no face appeared merely a blank emptiness, a headless ghost. Screaming, he fled and, the story goes, never raised a glass again!

Haunt of seasoned drinkers, the Cooperage on Newcastle Quayside possesses an ancient lineage, tracing its origins back to the thirteenth century. It is perhaps not surprising that some strange goings-on have been recorded and staff often feel they are 'not alone'. One otherwise sceptical and level-headed member working late and believing himself indeed alone, could not shake off a feeling of being watched. To his mounting panic he perceived a presence taking shape, inhuman, amorphous; terrifying. His cynicism fled, as did he. Restaurant staff occasionally report seeing the sad wraith of a long-haired girl and one cleaner had a truly frightening encounter with another indistinguishable, shrouded form which advanced, heavy with menace, until she near fainted on the spot.

8

BLOOD, SNOT & BILE

CURSE OF THE REIVERS

Essential to our understanding of these unique bandits cum guerrillas is our awareness of the society that built them. The land north *and* south of the border was a region of 'riding names', groups held together by the most powerful of all bindings – blood. Thus, not only was Northumberland subject to cross-border incursions from the Scots, but also to inter-clan raiding. Indeed, the border meant little to the reivers. In the words of a contemporary:

> The raiders from Newcastle, from Tynedale and from Redesdale were as much a nuisance to their compatriots as was anyone from over the Border. Indeed, at the time compatriot meant nothing and the Border did not count for much, for men who had made the place too hot to hold them on one side would flee to kinsmen and friends on the other, being Scottish when they will and English at their pleasure.

TO BE BE-REAVED

Reivers (from the old English meaning to rob) were not all 'outlaws', although some of them most certainly were. They came from all classes and backgrounds, having in common the ability to ride and to fight and the need to survive in a hostile environment. Marauding reivers carried out cattle-thieving raids with impunity, both across the border and on their neighbours, knowing that the rule of law simply did not apply in their homelands. It was an accepted way of life. Practising systematic thievery and destruction, they have the dubious distinction of bringing the word 'bereaved' to the English language, as indeed they did 'blackmail', another reiver practice.

> By the sixteenth century, robbery and blood feud had become
> virtually systematic, and that century saw the activities of the steel-
> bonneted border riders – noble and simple, robber and lawman,
> soldier and farmer, outlaw and peasant – at their height.

Surprisingly perhaps, these reivers were not indigenous to the borders.
During the fourteenth century, in an attempt to repopulate an area
made a dangerous economic desert by Anglo-Scots warfare, Edward
III of England and his counterpart in Scotland encouraged what we
would term 'relocation' to the border region. The people were chosen
quite deliberately as being capable of brutish and violent behaviour;
the settlers were brought in to form a protective 'pale' or bulwark
on either side. In exchange for land and low rents the monarch
required military service on demand. During times of conscription
by his country, the reivers would serve as 'prickers', light horsemen
with considerable skill at reconnoitering and armed engagement. The
area soon became heavily populated, a situation exacerbated by the
gavelkind inheritance system, which on his death divided a man's
land between his sons; the parcels of land thus handed down were too
small to provide an honest living:

> This state of affairs, combined with a lack of legitimate alternative
> occupations, soon gave rise to an ever-growing delinquent element
> in Border society. Theft became endemic.

A CLIMATE FOR KILLING

So, an idea that had appeared to have merit went seriously awry. Like
Frankenstein's creature, it developed a life of its own, with disastrous
effects. These rough incomers established what we know as reiver
practices and made the border into an area that the author, in his
previous work *Border Fury*, likens to war-torn Bosnia in the 1990s.
The unique provenance and nature of the reivers probably accounts
for the need for defensive buildings along this border; no such
building for domestic protection appears on the Anglo-Welsh border.
It is important to recognise that the people who built the towers and
bastles (fortified blockhouses also called 'peles') were the same people
who attacked the homes of others:

Although they were cattle-stealers when the opportunity offered, [these men] were for most of the time farmers, and not very different from the men they robbed . . . Thus they had as much need as their victims for buildings which would hold them and their stock in safety.

In other words, we are not talking here about a set of villains who were perpetually attacking their peace-loving countrymen. Reiving was the principal business of everyone in the region; it was simply a way of earning a living during the reiving 'season' of late August to February whenever the weather and skies allowed:

A foray might involve a dozen riders or half a thousand, with the graynes active every night the weather allowed, the bright reivers' moon their guiding star. So important was this lunar conspiracy that the image appears in border heraldry – the Scotts' badge was a star and two crescent moons; mottoes such as 'we'll have moonlight again' were popular amongst riding names.[*]

[*] Sykes, J., Latimer J. & Fordyce, T., *Local Records,* 4 vols (Newcastle upon Tyne 1833–76)

THE ENGLISH DISEASE

For some time Scotland appeared immune from the ravages of that great pandemic known as the Black Death. It would appear that a body of Scottish reivers, raiding into Northumberland, carried the contagion back with them, thus the plague became more British than purely English. It is highly unlikely any on England's northern frontier were unduly dismayed. Boccaccio witnessed the effects of the great pestilence at first hand:

In men and women alike, it first betrayed itself by the emergence of certain tumours, in the groin or the armpit, some of which grew as large as a common apple – from the said parts of the body the deadly disease soon began to propagate and spread itself in all directions.

This terrible curse, which seemed like the very wrath of God, originated in Asia, carried by rats and passed on by fleas which drank of the rodents' infected blood, reached Dorset by sea in 1348 and, for a year, ravaged the land, killing anywhere between 30 and 40 per cent of the population.

A VERY BLACK DEATH

The disease was termed 'Black' after the blackened blood which swelled from tumours or buboes. Death, and a painful one at that, normally ensued within 24 hours. Other variants were septicaemia, a form of blood poisoning, or pneumonia which attacked the lungs; both were deadly. Contagion spread like wildfire through crowded chares and reeking tenements – the poor and hungry had little defence and there was no remedy. Terror and death stalked Newcastle's streets; nor were the country areas any safer, whole communities succumbed, leaving only their traces upon maps.

'Bring out your dead' – a doleful cry that has entered our folk memory – would have resounded through city streets during this dreadful visitation. Nor was it the only time Newcastle would be cursed; there was at least a hand-span of outbreaks before the fourteenth century ended. Normal funerary practice could simply not keep up with numbers of fatalities. Last rites, so important to medieval men and women, were frequently if not invariably impossible to administer. Mass graves were dug and as quickly filled, normal urban life and trade could not continue, the rich fled city streets for isolation and possible sanctuary in the shire.

COUNTING THE COST

How many people died locally is impossible to estimate. Population levels in 1400 were estimated at 4,000 – so this might imply thatanywhere from 1,000 to 1,500 had succumbed, hardly any families within the crowded centre would have been spared. We know that at Monkseaton, now in North Tyneside, that bondage (tenanted) holdings were reduced by a third, by 1377 six out of ten farms had been vacant 'since the first pestilence'. Belford, which had previously interred its dead at Bamburgh, needed a cemetery of its own, so great was the mortality.

Religious life in the county was also hard hit. It has been estimated that as many as half and even more of parish priests succumbed and, for the monasteries in the shire, their position was already badly eroded through Scottish raiding. The nunnery at Holystone was temporarily abandoned, impoverished and terrorised, granges were torched and beasts lifted. The smaller nunnery at Guyzance disappears from record during the first half of the fourteenth century and these calamities exacerbated the steady decline of monastic houses. In many cases only a shell remained when the final blow fell at the dissolution.

KING CHOLERA

During later centuries urban expansion and a swelling population bred opportunities for disease. The aged, cramped and squalid closes of the Quayside and Westgate were especially prone. Although smallpox vaccination had been available since the early nineteenth century, outbreaks remained commonplace. Between June 1824 and the following February some 1,100 cases of the sickness are mentioned with nearly 20 per cent leading to death. In the filthy, overcrowded and unsanitary tenements, contagion was a regular bedfellow – 'the fever districts' as they were known.

Through the early decades of the nineteenth century, Typhus was endemic, with over 100 cases a year. As populations swelled and accommodation did not, the incidence multiplied – by 1845 it is said there were no fewer than 772 reported cases.

Cholera was a relative newcomer with a series of truly terrifying epidemics ravaging the whole country. The first major 'visitation' during 1831–2 may have killed as many as 80,000 people nationwide. One of those who perished in Newcastle during the first outbreak was distinguished historian Aeneas Mackenzie; some 306 citizens in total died. During the second visitation of 1848–9 another 412 lives were lost with 1,533 people succumbing during the third in 1853.

This new and terrifying disease spread panic and emergency steps were required. The corporation appointed a Board of Health, isolation hospitals were thrown up, theatres, balls, assemblies were banned, ships were quarantined and soldiery confined to their lines.

Reeking chares were washed down with a hot lime mix and landlords were exhorted to cleanse their crammed tenements (this expense could be passed on to tenants of course); nobody was proposing a social upheaval along Chartist lines.

One doleful and oft-repeated sight was tumbrels bearing the many dead. Fatalities had to be interred within the day, and not taken inside churches, so great was the risk of contagion. Graves needed to be deep with quick lime thrown in. Sykes, in his *Local Records*, gives an eyewitness account of the terror:

> It was most distressing . . . to hear during the greatest fatality of the disorder the constant tolling of the bells of the churches from morn to night. To witness: in rapid succession such a number of corpses being conveyed through the streets, many of them without a single attendant except the man leading the horse and he, holding the bridle at its utmost stretch.

PUBLIC HEALTH – A NEW ELIXIR

'King' Cholera was the prompt for fresh awareness of the importance of public hygiene. Clean streets, fresh water and functioning sanitation was a far more effective remedy to disease than medical responses alone, prevention was infinitely preferable to cure. Fears of a further Cholera outbreak in 1848, as contagion and revolution spread over Europe, finally spurred the reformers in parliament to act, passing the first Public Health Act. Despite the glaring deficiencies in the current, unhappy state, reform was not popular – too many vested interests were perceived to be at risk and Shaftesbury and the 'do-gooders' struggled.

This first great public health crusade produced little tangible improvement. In Newcastle, despite the ravages of the disease, responses were muted. During that traumatic Year of Revolutions the corporation merely threw up some ad hoc public baths and wash houses on New Road, past Keelman's Hospital. The old church burial grounds were finally closed down six years later but it required the more effective public health legislation of 1872 and 1875 to fully prime the reform process.

STORM AND TEMPEST

Most inhabitants of Newcastle and south Northumberland remember only too vividly the floods of September 2008 when Morpeth, particularly, was very hard-hit, significant portions of the town being inundated. Such cataclysms, though mercifully rare, are not unknown. The great fire of 1248 consumed the old Norman Bridge over the Tyne in Newcastle, constructed in about 1175 from timber. A fine stone crossing was thrown across as the town recovered, though this still utilised those original stone piers which had withstood the conflagration, dating from the time of the first Roman bridge. The new structure was part defensible, with stout gatehouses at both ends and a central tower, latterly used as cells for 'lewd and disorderly persons'.

If it still stood today, it would be guaranteed ample custom over an average weekend! The bridge was a busy thoroughfare in its own right; complete with timbered dwellings clinging like limpets to the parapets and a chapel of St Thomas the Martyr on the northern side. A swelling flood in 1339 swept much of this superstructure away but the foundations survived and the various accretions were rebuilt. Pandon, at this point quite an important suburb inhabited by the rising urban bourgeoisie, suffered very badly. Timber-framed houses, sunk on piles, were destroyed as the river and Pandon Burn jointly rose in fearsome spate.

THE GREAT FLOOD

By the latter part of the eighteenth century the now-ancient bridge had become a major retail space and perilously cantilevered structures swung dizzyingly from the over-burdened parapets. November 1771 opened with a constant downpour; by the middle part of the month river waters were swirling, black and leaden, around the venerable piers. At around 2.00 a.m. on the 17th the central arch of the bridge gave way, timbered dwellings flung like matchwood upon the huge and surging waters which had swallowed whole areas of Quayside on both banks. The storm-capped surge was littered with broken spars and timbers, cordage, canvas, the smashed hulls of river-craft and bodies of those drowned.

DELIVERANCES

A Mr Fiddes, whose shop and home clung to the shattered span, managed to lead his family and servants in the howling dark, over the tottering portion that still stood, demonic winds rocking those piers still holding. His maid, when they had reached safety on the Gateshead side, begged her employer to return with her and retrieve her bundle of worldly goods before the rest gave way. Amazingly, Fiddes agreed and the pair, foolhardily, set off on their quixotic mission. Fate is best left untempted for this time they'd come once too often and the remaining piers gave way; both drowned.

Geordie Woodford, bricklayer, was on the shore observing a desperate huddle of survivors, the Weatherley family, clinging to one of the surviving abutments, the span on either side having given way. Their plight was dire and immediate for this precarious refuge was visibly disintegrating. Quick-witted Geordie, however, had spotted that some of the cantilevered beams survived and that he might use these as a set of rungs to reach those trapped. Undeterred by the mounting storm, lashing the flimsy beams, flinging scraps of partitions into the rising flood, he edged out and pulled each of the family back to safety, seemingly oblivious to the barrage of nature's fury. No lives were lost and Geordie, deservedly, became a local hero.

Mr Patten, the general dealer, found himself, his family and staff, sweeping majestically towards the river mouth, as his house fell whole into the torrent. Speed and the lightweight timber construction kept this unlikely ark afloat. Helpless, the detached dwelling with its unwilling passengers sailed past Walker, Wallsend and Hebburn to finally ground on Jarrow Slakes, majestically stranded on the bare expanse of featureless mud flats. Miraculously all within emerged unscathed – even the family pets! Despite the scale of destruction, only six people were in fact drowned altogether but the bridge was totally demolished. It required a further decade before a replacement was completed; a rather handsome Georgian structure which stood until it was replaced by Armstrong's famous Swing Bridge in 1873 (in the basement area of Watergate building on the Newcastle side, two ribbed arches from the medieval structure can still be viewed, last survivors of the original dozen).

THE GREAT FIRE OF 1854

Fire was a constant threat in urban settlements with tightly-packed lanes of multi-storeyed timber-framed dwellings. Much of the medieval town was consumed by the earlier great fire in 1248 but it is the events of 6 October 1854 that have endured most potently in folk-memory. The mid-nineteenth-century Quayside was a Tolkienesque huddle of decayed timber-framed tenements, most given over to warehousing, professional offices and ale houses. Here, the history of the city was writ in that noisome warren of chares and rookeries, the elegant rise of All Saints' crowning the disordered huddle clustered below. Across the slow sweep of river, on the Gateshead side, a brutalist array of bunker-like warehouses crammed the waterfront.

Behind these blunt façades the materials for what would now be termed an improvised explosive device of biblical proportions were stored, the stuff of Armageddon – sulphur, naptha, nitrate of soda and manganese spread over the seven floors of what had been Bertram's Warehouse. Next to this lay Wilson's Worsted Factory, at this point brim full of woolsacks adjacent to substantial vats of

oil – highly flammable of course. Behind these, on the landward side across the narrow breadth of Hillgate, there stood a series of clinging, overcrowded tenements which rose like a series of breakers up the dense slope toward St Mary's Church.

In the small hours of 6 October the ancient churchyard was crowded with residents who'd struggled from their beds as the alarm had been raised. Wilson's was on fire, flames already curling and leaping from the fortress-like structure. The graveyard, with its elevated position, offered a proper grandstand, as did the rigging of ships moored on both sides. After all, a really good blaze was something to see.

FANNING THE FLAMES

Others were more actively engaged including the North British Fire Brigade; soldiers from 26th Foot (Cameronians) under Lieutenant Paynter; Mr Haggie, Gateshead's Mayor; William Woods, director of the Newcastle Fire Office whose materials were stored in Bertram's; and Bertram himself. One celebrity spectator was Alexander Dobson, son of the celebrated architect who, with a cadre of swells, had a bird's eye view from a gantry crowning Davidson's tall mill. Despite

the energy and enthusiasm of this eclectic mix of fire-fighters, the furnace heat was proving intolerable and Bertram's was soon aflame; a great funnel of burning sulphur, lighting the autumn skies, began to spill from the upper levels. Paynter and his platoon were forced to give ground, retreating into Church Walk.

It was now very nearly three in the morning: the scene was instantly and cataclysmically transformed by a colossal explosion as the Gateshead side erupted in a huge blast engulfing the entire area. The apocryphal flash and bang were heard and seen as far south as Northallerton! Two firemen, Joseph Todd and Martin Hall, were trapped by falling debris then horribly immolated in a cascade of fiery sulphur. Lieutenant Paynter died when crushed by tumbling masonry and young Dobson and his fellow watchers from the mill gantry were hurled bodily into the flames. Most of the residents of Hillgate Lodging house perished as the structure was simply demolished by the blast, whipped away as though by a hurricane.

CRESCENDO

And, as though borne by hurricane winds, a vast lethal spray of debris showered over the river to strike the Newcastle side like a meteor storm. All of the gas lighting was snuffed out, one man was decapitated and his severed head sent spinning into the flame-lit waters. A new source of light flickered and then swelled as hungry flames licked at the wooden frames, ancient dried timbers that caught like brushwood and, like brush fire, the conflagration took instant hold. Most available crews had been serving on the Gateshead bank. Many were now dead or disabled and frantic telegraph messages summoned fire-fighters from all over the north. South Shields water tender was soon on the scene but it was, from the start, an unequal battle. Newcastle's Quayside, nearly a thousand years of history, was being hungrily consumed. All of those ancient wynds – Grindon, Pallister's, Peppercorn, Colvin's, Blue Anchor and Hornsby's – were sucked into the deepening void.

Morning revealed a scene of utter devastation, as though the very wrath of God had seared both banks. On the Gateshead side, a 40ft crater marked the epicentre of the frightful blast. Seven-year-old Jimmy Nicholson's broken body was recovered from beneath the headstone which, flung like pebble, had crushed him. Most fire-fighters had simply disappeared or their charred remains proved impossible to identify. Many hundreds had suffered dreadful injuries and a casualty clearing station was established in the Fishmarket annexe to the shattered Guildhall, like a scene from the Western Front sixty years on. Chief Fire Officer Isaac Anderson was among those injured and he, like many others, succumbed to his terrible burns. In all, the official death toll stood at 53 though it is likely that numerous others died in the Hillgate Lodging House and went unrecorded; roughly 800 people were made homeless.

OUT FROM THE RUBBLE

Amid the devastation there were some remarkable escapes. One couple in Oakwellgate were awoken by the blast and leapt out of bed, barely had they risen when debris smashed through their roof and destroyed the bed on which they'd been sleeping. On the day after, a lone fireman was freed alive from the rubble, a child survived by adopting the handy expedient of hiding in the earth closet or 'netty'. Mayor Haggie who had been in the thick of the action also miraculously survived. As the flames roared and spread, the mayor had swapped places with Councillor Pattison from Westgate Ward so he could check how matters stood elsewhere. When the explosion occurred Haggie threw himself under the hull of a fire tender and, despite the deadly avalanche of tumbling masonry, was pulled free, unhurt, by a police officer. Pattison, who had taken his place, was killed instantly.

Today, of course, both quaysides have changed beyond all recognition; perhaps the most telling survivor is St Mary's Church, no stranger to several damaging fires. The place is now a superbly realised heritage centre and contains some excellent photographs and records of the Great Fire, highly commended to the visitor.

THE TOWN MOOR EXPLOSION, 1867

One of Newcastle's most distinguished sons of the industrial age was the chemist John Mawson (1815–67). A Cumbrian by birth he trained in Sunderland before opening premises in Mosley Street during his late twenties. The site of the homeopathic dispensary, located on Hood Street, which he acquired, would become the site of Mawson, Swan & Morgan (latterly Waterstone's and now yet another clothing emporium). Swan, inventor of the electric incandescent lamp, entered into partnership with him in 1865.

Two years later Mawson was appointed as sheriff and one of the matters he inherited was the tricky business of nine canisters of nitro-glycerine, at that time stored within the cellar of the White Swan in Cloth Market. Nitro was highly volatile and this quantity had the equivalent blast to four tons of black powder! Nobody was overly-anxious to assume responsibility for so deadly a load and when a warrant for its removal was finally issued, Mawson was consulted. His solution was to dispose of the liquid explosive by pouring the contents of each canister down one of the old mine workings on Town Moor.

The first half-dozen, with Mawson in attendance, were duly emptied but the remaining three were found to have crystallised. While the party deliberated, one of the canisters (nitro was notoriously unstable) simply exploded annihilating and obliterating five of the watchers. Both Mawson and Bryson, town surveyor, were fatally injured and soon succumbed to their terrible injuries. The nearby fever or isolation hospital was badly damaged, so potent was the blast. Over 2,000 mourners followed Mawson's cortège, shops were closed and thousands more lined the route to Jesmond cemetery, the city had lost one of its most talented sons.

9

HOWAY THE LADS! THIS SPORTING LIFE

'Howay the lads' I hord him shoot
Ower the baying of the mob
We're the black and white army
And wiv come te shut yer gob
Ye can tell yer ma when ye get hyem
The toon did wallop ye
He danced a jig and waved his arms
Eyes filled up with glee
'Lets be havin ye noow' He cried
As the baal went true of aim
'Divint gis a Mackem whinge cos
Sunderland's lost the game'
'The Fan' by Irv Graham

THE TOON

The local derby rivalry with Sunderland (aka 'the Black Cats'), two fanatical bands of supporters, is synonymous with stripes – the black and white of Newcastle against the red and white of Sunderland. This was not always the case. Sunderland originally played in blue and, worse, prior to 1894, Newcastle played in red.

Women have been trying to get a foothold in the sport for a long time, with mixed success until recently. The 'Munitionettes' took their names from the munitions factories where most them were employed during and after the First World War. Young and full of energy, despite 12-hour days, 500 of them set up their own football teams and used competitions to raise money for charity. They played at least 26 games at St James' Park among numerous other venues. They attempted to play on after the war but in 1921 the Football Association banned women's football from their grounds. That ban would take a full fifty years to lift.

Cardinal Basil Hume was born in the City and never lost his connection to Newcastle including a lifelong passion for Newcastle United. He used to tell the story of his meeting with Jackie Milburn. Both men it seems were in awe of each other; both suggested (after a long and awkward silence) an autograph. And both stood there waiting for the other, more famous and important person, to oblige.

St James' Park nearly became a World Cup venue in 1966 (yes, it could have happened here). However, a spat between the council and the board of Newcastle United prevented this happening and the honour went to Middlesbrough. Oddly enough, the two main figures involved were also political opponents: T. Dan Smith was Labour leader of the Council while United Chairman William McKeag was a proper Tory.

Current capacity of the ground, following a number of building phases from the 1920s onwards, is 52,387 making it the seventh largest in the country. However, the biggest gates do not necessarily require the biggest grounds. Newcastle experienced their greatest average turnout (over 56,000) for three years in the late 1940s and their all-time record attendance was for a match against Chelsea in 1930 (68,386).

Three men are in contention for the shortest recorded time to score a goal in an English top-tier football match; two of them were Newcastle players. The fastest Premiership goal on record is held by Tottenham's Ledley King. Next, however, comes Alan Shearer, who scored 10.4 seconds after kick-off against Manchester City in January 2003. But the unofficial top place could go to Jackie Milburn who is believed to have scored after just 6 seconds against Cardiff in November 1947.

A further, more recent statistic: the first time anyone in the Premier League has been 4–0 down at half time, yet recovered enough to manage a draw took place here. In February 2011, Arsenal seemed to have Newcastle United well beaten at the break, but United battled back to level terms in the second half.

LIVESTOCK

Newcastle has had its share of sports we would not tolerate today.

The Garrison Room in Castle Keep houses a stone circle set with an iron ring which many visitors assume was used to tether prisoners. It was actually an anchor for cattle used in bull-baiting, a practice positively encouraged by local butchers who thought a decent baiting tenderised the meat. The bull got its own back the last time baiting took place at Sandhill where the stone was found in 1768. Kenlyside Henzell risked more than his apprentice's allowance to make a wager as the bull gored him fatally. Baiting went on until 1835.

Cock fighting was banned in 1849 but was easily perpetuated in cockpits down seedy back streets and the yards of public houses. What was thought to be the last active cockpit in England was closed by down by police when they discovered a site at Gallowgate in 1874.

And, right in the centre of the city, is a monument to somebody who in his time was hailed as a fervent 'cocker' (yes, that really was the name for those many respectable gentlemen who followed the sport). Earl Grey has all sorts of achievements mentioned but his skill as a bird breeder is not among them.

GOLF

Charles I is said to have enjoyed a daily game of golf throughout his imprisonment in Newcastle during the English Civil War. A plaque at Shieldfield, where he is said to have played, commemorates his passion and one of the nearby tower blocks is named after him.

Golf, like most other sports in the region, was largely dominated by men until well into the twentieth century. This might account for the targeting of Gosforth Golf Club by suffragettes during their bombing and arson campaign of 1913. A policeman on his rounds found the bomb (with a burnt-out fuse) near the clubhouse. Benton Club did not escape so lightly. A number of greens were dug up and labels inserted: 'Business before pleasure, Wanted: chivalrous golfers, apply Lincoln's Inn.'

Another golf club had been established on Town Moor in 1891 with its headquarters in the old mill on Claremont Road (you can still see the inscription above the door). It was not entirely successful. The greens had to be enclosed to keep cattle off but well-heeled members had to put up with a distinctly less affluent club next door (Newcastle United Workmen's Golf Club). Most of the gentlemen headed off to form Northumberland Golf Club in 1898 with the remainder setting up Gosforth in 1907.

At this point the Workmen's Club bought the mill headquarters for £13 and remained there until 1970.

RACING

Killingworth Moor hosted the annual Newcastle horse races from 1621 to 1721 (when the event shifted to Town Moor). Prizes of hats, cheese and tobacco were eagerly sought. 'Blaydon Races', the signature tune, is still associated with the cult of Geordie and is routinely sung at Newcastle United matches. It was first performed at

Balmbra's Music Hall in the Bigg Market at a testimonial evening for the famous rower, Harry Clasper. Not many ditties encompass that many sporting connections!

Just off the Town Moor is Grandstand Road, named after structures erected on the Moor to facilitate racing. One of the smaller ones, constructed in 1867, was by William Parnell, the same architect who designed the Tyne Opera House. These were select facilities; the vast majority of race-goers occupied the infield of an otherwise unfenced course. On Northumberland Plate days (which commenced in 1833), thousands would cram into a sea of tents, marquees and makeshift stands to gamble, drink and discourse. The noise must have been unbelievable and difficulties of keeping off the race track considerable.

Parnell's stand was dismantled and taken to the new race course at Gosforth Park when it opened in 1882. Clearly a sturdy construction, it went on in use until the Second World War.

RUGBY

This was another sport which took full advantage of open ground available alongside the Town Moor and out at Gosforth. Northern Football Club, formed at Elswick by a pair of printers, was initially organised from the Mill Inn on Westgate Road – now long since closed. The club established itself at McCracken Park in 1937 and has been there ever since.

Not far away, on what is now the Greystoke Park Estate, Gosforth RFC was established. The team would achieve a national reputation, eventually forming their professional wing into Newcastle Falcons who now play from the old Newcastle Chronicle and Journal Sports ground at Kingston Park, while the amateur wing has moved to Woolsington.

WHERE WOULD YOU FIND A RUGBY CLUB DECORATED WITH THE SYMBOL OF HEALING?

The rod of Asclepius, Greek God of healing, is part of the motif of Medical Rugby Football Club in Heaton (known simply as 'the Medicals'). This crest decorates their stand, built in 1933 and which remains in use. The club itself has been in existence since 1898.

GET YOUR SKATES ON

Some modern sports are perhaps not so new after all. Roller skating enjoyed a heyday from the 1870s until the beginning of the First World War. A large rink – 300ft long – was created on Town Moor next to the old Grandstand. So massive was the corrugated iron building that it was converted to an aircraft factory when Armstrong Whitworth bought the empty shell in 1913.

The site had another use after the war. The factory was demolished in 1920 and Moor Court flats were constructed on the site, complete with a court for another early twentieth-century sport – squash. This had originally been played in the racquet court in College Street and now needed a larger home.

At the same time ice skating was becoming extremely popular. Lakes such as that in Leazes Park could be frozen over during the winter to allow outdoor skating; something we might otherwise think of as a modern phenomenon indulged in outside the Centre for Life around Christmas time.

WHICH SPORT DID THE IRISH BRING TO TYNESIDE?

Handball: hammering a small, tightly stuffed ball against a wall may not sound terribly exciting but the stakes were. Men would bet a week's wages on the result and many a local woman would end up wishing the Temperance Movement would succeed in eradicating it along with the drinking sessions that accompanied it. The sport was played by all ages. Buddle Board School (now an arts centre) still has a wall which was specially extended and buttressed to provide playing space for the sport.

BOXING CLEVER

The growth of heavy industry mirrored the growth in all kinds of sport in the north-east, boosting a population in search of entertainment and with handsome wages in pocket. Miners were reputed to be among the most enthusiastic supporters for any activity, especially those involving a bet or two.

Hundreds of them responded to a handbill announcing a combat at the Forth Pleasure Gardens in 1799. The stated date might have offered a warning – 1 April – and when local commentator M.A. Richardson suggested that the fake match was an attempt by local pub landlords to boost business by providing sorrows to drown, he may very well have been right!

The sport was enormously popular; there were 38 boxing rings in Newcastle in 1933 with the most famous at St James' Hall opposite the football ground, capable of holding over 4,000 spectators.

There were up to six boxing matches a week at the zenith of popularity as well as wrestling bouts. The latter continued after boxing ceased in 1967, although by the time it finally closed in 1976 it was reduced mainly to bingo.

KEEPING UP

Cycling, in particular racing, was not regarded as respectable in its earlier days. Nonetheless, a dozen north-east clubs were formed in the 1870s, and some of them made use of Wallers at Dalton Street in Byker. A cinder track and grandstand had been built by Newcastle professional George Waller, using his winnings from an endurance race in 1879. He did 10,500 circuits of a London agricultural show hall (near 1,400 miles in total) – they took the sport seriously, these early cyclists. All Saints' cemetery houses the grave of one of them,

Harry Carr. His cycle decorates one side of the stone, his club badge the other – and we thought that kind of kitsch was modern!

RUNNING

Amateur running clubs (as opposed to the earlier nineteenth-century professionals) developed in the 1880s; some, like Elswick Harriers, are still going today.

Newcastle is, of course, the starting point for the Great North Run. This renowned half marathon has taken place since 1981 and continues to raise large amounts of money for charity. Early winners of the race include a member of Elswick Harriers. However, participation has always been diverse. Mo Mowlam, during her time as a lecturer at Newcastle University took part and was pictured in a local newspaper as she recovered at the end of the race; 'not my most dignified moment' was how she described it.

CRICKET

There would be no 'Toon' without cricket. Where did football develop in the north-east? Why, at the cricket grounds which had sprung up to take advantage of opportunities for league play offered by the coming of the railways. The two clubs which made up Newcastle FC both began in this way. Stanley Cricket Club in Byker formed East End FC while West End Junior Cricket Club gave rise to West End FC with their HQ somewhere called St James' Park.

We tend to think of cricket as a game for the village green or suburban club. In Newcastle it was a city centre pastime with a substantial ground on what is now Northumberland Road, facing City Baths.

Northumberland County Cricket club moved to Jesmond Ground on Osborne Road in 1897, inheriting as their pavilion a leftover chalet built for the great exhibition held on Town Moor.

It is not known if this was the chalet from which waitresses in Swiss costume served light teas, but we do know the next occupants were policemen, Osborne Road was originally the Constabulary Ground. It is safe to assume they stuck to the rules.

This ad hoc structure was replaced by a new pavilion in 1963 which has been used by the likes of Len Hutton, Garry Sobers and Viv Richards. That international reputation came in useful when the future of the ground came into question in 2003. A campaign to save it resulted in the establishment of Newcastle Cricket Club, the lease of the ground itself going to Royal Grammar School. Now used as a venue for community cricket, Jesmond has twice won a north-east ground of the year award – howzat?

South Northumberland Cricket Club, based in Gosforth, is one of the oldest clubs in the area. Founded in 1864, the members moved to their current pitch in 1892. There have been some notable changes since then, including selling off part of the ground for housing development in order to raise money. Proceeds were invested in the future; Newcastle Cricket Centre, attached to the ground, provides facilities and development space for aspiring players and amateurs and has amply demonstrated its high standard when used by the England squad.

One of those early cricket players might find it odd to visit a modern ground. A recent excursion to the clubhouse was notable for a spectacle of avid cricket fans keeping an eye on England's football team on TV while watching a one-day match outside. The international team playing were arrayed in brightly coloured sweat suits, complete with helmets while a hog roasted happily alongside the pitch. Not quite cricket whites on the village green perhaps, but the place was humming with enthusiasm.

TENNIS

Newcastle has more than its share of unusual tennis facilities. The now empty Racquets Court on College Street was built for members of the Union Club on Westgate Road (these days, a pub). We are remarkable in that we still possess a Real Tennis Club. This version of the game has a long and noble history. There is Real Tennis at Hampton Court where it is believed Henry VIII liked to play.

Lawn tennis also has a home in Newcastle. This sport took off in the 1870s and swiftly demoted croquet to second place as the sport for the middle classes and women in particular.

BOWLING

The creation of public parks saw an expansion of interest in bowling as aficionados of the sport petitioned for space. The city's first municipal bowling green was located in Brandling Park but they rapidly appeared in other green spaces as well. The initial county association for bowls – the Northumberland and Durham Bowling Association – was formed from park clubs.

Newcastle remains unusual in the amount of public space (as opposed to private grounds) devoted to bowling. If you put all our bowling greens together you would have enough space to house St James' Park 26 times over.

WHERE IS THE STADIUM THAT NEVER WAS?

Byker: a cinder track runs alongside the playground created from a rubbish tip in the Warwick Street area. In the 1950s plans were laid to build a gigantic stadium, big enough to hold nearly 100,000 spectators. There was to be for football, cycling, running, etc. They even had an opening event in 1955 to christen the cinder track and a wee pavilion. But somehow, the £250,000 they needed to do the job turned into millions – unavailable millions.

10

IMAGES OF TYNESIDE

A COUPLE OF GEORDIE FLICKS

In the cold depths of January 2011, the writers spent three days working with a local film company to recreate the Siege of Newcastle of 1644 – not from the lofty reaches of the keep but from the more rural location of Aydon Castle near Corbridge. A splendid almost fairytale fortified manor, perched several hundred feet above the slab-sided gorge of the Cor Burn, its narrow accessible frontage is dominated by a strong curtain wall. Aydon looks every inch the border *fortalice*. The transformation, in numbing cold, to the appearance of late summer within and without the beleaguered walls of the besieged city, required both art and artifice. December 2010 was marked by extensive and heavy snowfall, though finally the snow had cleared and arctic blue skies at least afforded a pure, clean light. Arpeggio Films from Byker made the film for Tyne and Wear Museums to accompany the Discovery Museum's Civil Wars exhibition. Visitors would thus experience well-realised images of their city at war, almost a forgotten footnote in the history of the period.

Geordies always have the impression that southerners view both them and their beloved city as being uncouth; a land of outside netties, flat caps, wife-beating and dog-baiting. By and large, however, Geordie is not unhappy with this image and the film depiction which he most reveres, *Get Carter* (see p. 171), is singularly bleak and uncompromising, a dour northern empire of petty crooks, gangsters and slot machines. Much of what formed dramatic backdrops for the Mike Hodges film has now gone and the cityscape has been radically transformed but the hard-man image Michael Caine so chillingly conveys still finds ample resonance.

ANDY CAPP

The late Reginald Smythe (1917–98) created perhaps the most potent image of the working class or non-working northern man with Andy Capp who featured, from 1957, in both the *Daily* and *Sunday Mail*. Andy, long-term unemployed, and his long suffering wife Flo, came from Smythe's native Hartlepool rather than Newcastle (a bronze statue of Andy, complete with his signature flat cap, was unveiled there in June 2007).

THE LITTLE WASTER

'The dole is my shepherd, I shall not work' is just one of hundreds of one-liners from Andy's real life counterpart, comedian Robert Michael ('Bobby') Thompson (1911–88), better known as the 'little waster'. The vertically challenged Bobby was in fact a native of Fatfield, Washington, which implies he was more of a Wearsider. His strong accent, laced with Pitmatic (a near extinct blend of dialogue, particularly associated with south-east Northumberland mining districts), was a trademark which guaranteed renown within the region but prevented his career as a stand-up comic from progressing any distance beyond. He was a master of self-deprecation and the mother-in-law joke; shabby woollen jumper, flat cap and omnipresent Woodbine were his inevitable attire. Thrice married, like Andy he had difficulties with drink and debt which, with failing health, blighted his later years. Still he attained near legendary status on the club circuit, though it is unlikely his robust humour and endless Woodbines would find favour today under the dead hand of political correctness.

Bobby Thompson – 'the Little Waster'.

RETURN OF THE LIKELY LADS

In 1976, a big-screen spin off from the *Likely Lads* series with Rodney Bewes and James Bolam was filmed largely on Tyneside; Greggs of Gosforth, the Beehive pub at Earsdon, high-rise flats at Howdon, the Tyne Bridge and Grainger Market all featured. Twenty-four years later the immensely successful *Billy Elliot*, which grossed thirty-four times its production budget was filmed in East Durham, set in the aftermath of the 1984 Miners' Strike.

VIEW FROM THE BRIDGES

Newcastle's most enduring popular image is that of the Tyne bridges, including the newest Millennium structure. In the post-war years the city moved from a decaying industrial giant, post-industrial dereliction to service sector centre, a transition only partially successful and the

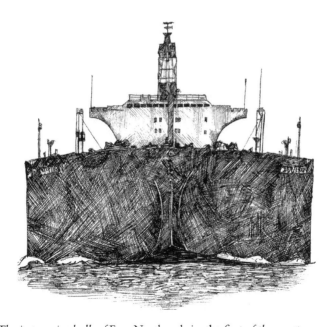

The impressive bulk of Esso Northumbria, **the** *first of the great supertankers, and the crowning achievement of the Tyneside shipyards.*

new prosperity has proved to be less securely bolstered than the old. The Angel of the North has joined the iconic pantheon in both local and external perspectives.

On 2 May 1969, the *Esso Northumbria* slid (if only just) into the water at Wallsend. She was the first of the giant supertankers, a vast leviathan of 126,000 tons. Named by Princess Anne, her launch became almost a defining moment for that generation of Tynesiders. The sheer size of the sea monster with its high raked stem and bulbous bow was a revelation, a tremendous feat of marine engineering, Swan Hunter's masterpiece. Yet within another generation shipbuilding had virtually gone. The great ship, stately and proud as she slid, groaningly into the ancient river is a potent image of what was seen as best and now lost.

FILM NOIR

Tyneside's introduction to film noir began quite early, prior to the Second World War in fact. Brian Hurst's *On the Night of the Fire* with Ralph Richardson and Diana Wynyard was released shortly after the outbreak. The dark and depressive nature of this film was out of sync with the more reassuring fare that wartime cinema-goers might need. Shot in Newcastle it is described as 'grim but gripping, a riveting psychological study.'

We see shots of the Tyne, Swing and Byker bridges and a tank is seen passing over the High Level. The lead couple take a Sunday walk along the Quayside market. Other locations are anonymous but appear to be close to the shipyards and river.

PAYROLL

Jumping forward to 1961, actor Michael Craig first appeared as heist leader Johnny Mellors in the 1961 black and white film *Payroll*. The view of the city portrayed was not intended to boost tourism – it was very gritty, working class and depressed, with post-war dereliction and industrial decay. This would now be considered as an archaic impression of Newcastle, to the extent the image has been coloured by nostalgia.

We see many shots of the bridges, the Central station and local transport of the 1960s. This is definitely another bit of noir and people still speculate on the exact location of the garage where the gang leave their car with a dying colleague.

GET CARTER

2011 marks the fortieth anniversary of perhaps the single most influential film to be shot on Tyneside – no perhaps about it really. *Get Carter*, released on 10 March 1971, has become the most iconic movie to be made in and around Newcastle. The choice of locations was determined by director Mike Hodges and the entire production went from concept to screen in just eight months with 40 days' intensive filming on Tyneside.

The original novel was set in a small unnamed steel-town near Doncaster (thought to be Scunthorpe) and Hull was planned as the original film location, but Hodges said that the visual drama of unreconstructed Newcastle just took his breath away.

So influential has the film become that the city's '*Get Carter* heritage' is a notable feature of the current opportunities on offer to visitors. The otherwise monstrously ugly and derelict Trinity Centre multi-storey car park in Gateshead enjoyed several stays of execution on no other grounds other than that it was a landmark location from the film. Fans can, from Gateshead Library, purchase their very own Berlin Wall style souvenir nugget of rubble from the demolished structure. The film was voted 16th of BFI's top 100 British films of the twentieth century in 1999 and is widely regarded as the best UK gangster movie of all time.

STORMY MONDAY

Seventeen years after Mike Hodges' directorial debut Carlisle-born Mike Figgis made his own with *Stormy Monday*. Club owner Finney, played by Tyneside music icon Sting, has a somewhat shady past which threatens to catch up with him when a group of US-based investors headed by the unscrupulous Cosmo (Tommy Lee Jones) propose to acquire his premises through intimidation.

The film which made good use of Quayside locations lacked the impact and durable appeal of *Get Carter* and critical reviews were muted. It certainly lacks the visceral punch its predecessor achieved thought it did spawn a 1990s TV series *Finney* with David Morrissey taking the Sting role and showing the character as a younger man and an unwilling participant in the local gangland scene, partly run by his murderously dysfunctional family and including Melanie Hill, a native of Sunderland and second wife of Sean Bean (who featured in the original film).

AND ALSO SHOWING

Mark Herman, in 2000, directed *Purely Belter* about a pair of teenagers struggling to fund season tickets for Newcastle United (ironically both young actors Chris Beattie and Greg McLane are from Sunderland). Topical matters such as domestic violence and child abuse are featured.

Two years later, and with a script by Peter Flannery, *The One and Only* a romantic comedy starred Richard Roxburgh, Patsy Kensit, Jonathan Cake and Justine Waddell. Directed by Simon Cellan Jones, the film offers a more upbeat view of Newcastle and was funded in part by the City Council. Although intended as comedy the action encounters matters of life and death, childlessness and adultery. The Angel of the North features as a potent and not infrequent totem.

In 2005 Danny Cannon directed *Goal* intended as the first in a series of three. It is a 'rags to riches' story of a young Hispanic football player who is spotted by a Newcastle United scout and eventually ends up playing for the 'Toon'. The hero has to undergo the stock tribulations but inevitably ends up scoring the vital goal to assure his place on the team – howay the lads!

HOME-GROWN

One of Tyneside's creative powerhouses and enduring successes has been Amber Films, founded in 1968:

The work is rooted in social documentary, built around long term engagements with working class and marginalised communities in the North of England. Through the gallery and cinema programs and at festivals and screenings, the group makes connections with inspirational production in the wider world. There is an integrated approach to production (which includes documentaries, dramas and photographic projects), publication (including exhibitions, books, DVDs and works created specially for the web) and distribution (though the odds sometimes seem to be stacked against it).

Amber has earned its considerable reputation by producing a series of first-rate social documentaries, focusing upon groups and communities in Tyneside and the region. Their many outstanding works include *Pursuit of Happiness* (2008) which became in part a eulogy for founder member Murray Martin who died the year before, and an outstanding Coalfield trilogy, focusing on the death of mining in East Durham (*The Sea, Like Father* and *Shooting Magpies*).

ON TELLY

It is perhaps surprising that Newcastle, with its wide, varied rural hinterland and sweeping coastline of wild sands and large skies, has not played host to more TV dramas. From 1976 to 1981 the BBC showed several series of James Mitchell's *When The Boat Comes In*, starring James Bolam and Susan Jameson. The former likely lad played Jack Ford, a First World War veteran who, in the grim recession of the 1920s, returns to a fictional northern town of Gallowshields. Mitchell, a prolific local author and screenwriter (who died in 2002) created the wonderfully down-at-heel assassin Callan, brought enduringly to life by Edward Woodward. Born in South Shields in 1926, the year of the General Strike, Mitchell was the son of a shipyard fitter, union activist and self-taught intellectual. As James Munro he penned a series of 1960s bond-type novels beginning with *The Man Who Sold Death* – his anti-hero was portrayed on screen by Stanley Baker.

Dick Clement and Ian La Frenais were the initial screenwriters for the highly successful comedy *Auf Wiedersehen, Pet* which ran for four series and some 40 episodes from 1983/1984, 1986 and 2002–4. The plot revolved around a group of seven UK construction workers who seek employment in Germany, reflecting economic trends of the time. Though the band members are drawn from across the UK, main focus is the three north-easterners.

It's a small world when it comes to north-east TV. Kevin Whately, one of the stars of *Auf Wiedersehen, Pet*, is married to Madeleine Newton, who played Dolly in *When the Boat Comes In*. The casting team of children's series *Geordie Racer* had not known they were actually married to each other when they were cast as Bev and Ray Hilton, parents of the young lead, Spuggy.

SPENDER

Jimmy Nail returned to his native Tyneside as tough copper *Spender* from 1991 to 1993 with Denise Welch and the late Sammy Johnson. The taciturn hero had been relegated back to the north-east from a career in the Met. A similar fate befell his successor Don Gilet, hero of *55 Degrees North*, which was shown in 2004. HMS *Calliope*, brick-built and landbound, served as HQ for the fictional 'Tyneside Police', Dervla Kirwan providing the love interest as smart CPS lawyer Claire Maxwell. Both series would suggest that Newcastle did not represent the career aspirations of rising police officers and that they only ended up back here when things went badly in London!

BYKER GROVE

Unquestionably one of the most successful series located on Tyneside was *Byker Grove*, created by Adele Rose and which ran between 1989 and 2006. The programme launched a number of media careers including those of Anthony McPartlin (P.J.) and Declan Donnelly (Duncan), now known better as Ant & Dec. Also, both Jill Halfpenny and Donna Air cut their TV stardom teeth in the series. Zenith produced the programme for BBC and it ran for a hefty 344 episodes.

Founder producer/director Matthew Robinson went on to become executive producer of *Eastenders*. Despite the title the actual location of the youth club was in Benwell; Zenith had purchased the 'Mitre' site (so named after the premises' previous life as pub and nightclub), and the property housed not just the actual set used for filming but production offices, wardrobe and make-up. After Zenith went into liquidation in 2007, Ant & Dec, through the medium of their own production company Gallowgate Productions Limited, are believed to have acquired the now-derelict site.

Perhaps one of the major factors which contributed towards *Byker Grove*'s success was that the storylines were far from anodyne and normal soap opera fare, and real themes such as drugs, child abuse, homelessness, teen pregnancy and abortion all featured. It was in November 1994 that the programme made headlines when two male characters were seen to kiss. The tabloids were shrill in their condemnation, calling for the producer's head but the challenging nature of such scenes won *Byker Grove* many supporters. It was not a comfortable series with leading characters insulated from harsh reality. Quite the reverse – P.J. is blinded in a paintball accident, another is electrocuted, one succumbs to a brain tumour, one is dispatched from this world to the next by a gas explosion, another is run over and one is paralysed by a fall.

THE REMARKABLE MARTINS

In the same week of July 1789 that the Bastille fell to a Parisian mob, John Martin was born in Haydon Bridge, Northumberland. He was the fourth son of a fencing-master who arranged for young John to be apprenticed to a coach builder in Newcastle. The arrangement did not prosper and Martin transferred his labours to the artist Bonifacio Musso, moving to London where he eked an uncertain existence. Each of the other Martin boys was remarkable – William the inventor, Richard the soldier and Jonathan who took the family eccentricity to new heights when he attempted to burn down York Minster, an offence which might have cost him his life.

John's sweeping works in oil, vast portentous biblical themes echo his place in the Northumbrian landscape. He achieved not inconsiderable success though never able to gain entry to the Royal Academy. Devoted to chess, fencing and the javelin he was much distracted by family tragedy and the cost of his brother's defence when Jonathan stood trial for arson following the York incident. His works, particularly 'Belshazzar's Feast' gained him a considerable following. Of a radical persuasion, he was nonetheless content to be patronised by royalty including the Russian Tsar, who gave him a gold medal. Like his brother William, to whose ideas he frequently gave form, he combined an interest in engineering with painting.

The family curse could not be avoided and, in his later years he suffered from manic depression, exacerbated by the suicide of Jonathan's son Richard. The Laing Art Gallery in Newcastle possesses a fine collection of Martin's work.

T.M. RICHARDSON JR

The sheer drama of Newcastle and its hinterland has proved a magnet for artists, including such titans as Turner. One of the most respected watercolourists from the area was Thomas Miles Richardson Junior (1813–90). He was a pupil of his artist father and first exhibited in London in 1832 – year of the great Reform Act. He established himself in the capital and was made an associate of the 'old' Society of Painters in Watercolours, being granted membership in 1851. Much of his output was inspired by dramatic mountainscapes in the Scottish Highlands and the Alps and he displayed a particular fondness for bright colours, using quantities of white heightening. Though a native Geordie, he never exhibited in Newcastle.

G.B. STICKS

George Blackie Sticks (1842–1900) was the son of an Edinburgh artist and became renowned as a painter of Northumbrian landscapes, though he also travelled widely throughout the highlands and English Lakes which feature in much of his mature work. As failing health curtailed his ability to travel he again refocused on local subjects. Though born in Edinburgh and into a family of artists, William Bell Scott (1811–90), having made a substantial reputation in London, secured a pioneering position as master of the government school of design in Newcastle, a post he held for two decades. His influence was considerable and his own output, perhaps most famously at Wallington Hall for Lady Trevellyan, considerable. He was a friend of Rossetti, and some of his verse (*Poems*, 1875) was illustrated by Sir Lawrence Alma-Tadema. Much of his time after 1870 was spent in London but his work in the academic sphere marked the genus of what would in time develop into Newcastle University.

TYNESIDE AT WAR

Some of the most striking and atmospheric images of Tyneside came from the lens of Cecil Beaton, better known of course for society portraits but who achieved mastery of the war-ravaged East End streets of London. In 1943, Beaton photographed Tyneside shipyards

One of Cecil Beaton's evocative wartime images of shipyard workers 'doing their bit'.

as a propaganda commission. His images, long overlooked, featured in a special exhibition from summer 2010 to summer 2011 at IWM North in Salford Quays. One shows a young female welder, proudly and self-consciously stood in front of half-finished ships, a living testament to women's role. Another gives us a young lad, dirt-grimed and ragged, yet infinitely purposeful in his labours. Overtly patriotic and jingoistic, it is still impossible for any native Geordie not to feel a stirring of pride – if we have to choose one enduring image then this would do splendidly.

THE CULLERCOATS COLONY

One of the area's better known artists was John Falconer Slater (1857–1937), who exhibited both locally and prolifically. Son of a corn mill owner, he worked as book-keeper for his father's business and prospected in the diamond fields before returning. A member of the Bewick School and North East Art Club, he is regarded as one of the best of the northern impressionists. For a number of years in his long life he was a member of the Cullercoats Colony. This remarkable ensemble of artistic talent thrived for half a century, between 1870 and 1920. Perhaps most celebrated was the American Winslow Homer who resided for a period in the Bay Hotel (demolished in 2005). Aside from Slater other colonists included Henry H. Emmerson, Robert Jobling, Arthur H. Marsh, Isa Thompson, John Charlton and Ralph Hedley.

11

ON THIS DAY IN
NEWCASTLE

8 January 1991
Spender with Jimmy Nail first aired.

17 January 1917
The present Royal Grammar School building opened (the school was founded in about 1477).

16 February 2010
An extension to the 1977 city centre shopping complex, Eldon Square, named St Andrew's Way opened, making this the largest UK city centre retail scheme.

21 February 1941
It was announced that Newcastle had made the largest contribution per head of population to British Red Cross and St John 'Penny-a-week' Fund during 1940.

25 February 1928
The Tyne Bridge, most iconic of the Tyne crossings, was opened.

28 February 1942
Newcastle and Gosforth Warship Week was inaugurated.

7 March 1829
Jane 'Jin' Jameson was hanged for the murder of her mother.

7 March 1942
In the BBC feature *Life over Here*, North America heard the story of the founding and working of the Northumberland and Durham War Needs Fund – the largest organisation of its kind in Britain.

10 March 1971
Mike Hodges' film *Get Carter* was first released in the UK.

15 March 1941
The Services Cup Final was held at St James' Park.

27 March 1940
The Lord Mayor received a letter from the Polish Ambassador in London thanking the city for its kindness to Poles stranded here during to the war.

27 March 1942
The first wartime Day Nursery was opened at Ashfield House by Dame Sybil Thorndike.

7 April 1943
The king and queen visited Tyneside and went to Byker and Heaton.

9–10 April 1941

More than 50 bombers caused widespread damage and 300 troops were used to fight resulting fires. Homes were damaged as well as Cambridge Street School, Bell Terrace School and St Michael's R.C. Church.

12 April 1944

Newcastle and Gosforth 'Salute the Soldier' week was inaugurated.

16 April 1988

Death of comedian Bobby Thompson – 'the Little Waster' (born 1911).

22 April 1988

Stormy Monday went on release.

25 April 1941

Air raid at 9.45 p.m. nine high explosive bombs, a shower of incendiaries and a parachute mine fell on Shields Road, Jesmond Vale, Heaton Park, Grace Street, Heaton Road and Guildford Place. 47 people were killed, 23 seriously injured, 47 slightly injured and 16 houses and shops demolished and 300 damaged.

28 April 1951

Jackie Milburn scored both goals in Newcastle United's 2–0 win over Blackpool in the FA Cup.

2 May 1969

The launch of the *Esso Northumbria,* built by Swan Hunter, took place.

3 May 1952

Newcastle won the FA Cup again, beating Arsenal 1–0.

7 May 1955

Jackie Milburn again scored at Wembley to beat Manchester City 3–1.

13 May 1945

A victory parade. was held.

15 May 1464
Wars of the Roses: Battle of Hexham, executions at Newcastle following the Lancastrian defeat, this battle brought the War in the North, 1461–4, to a close.

15 May 1943
Newcastle and Gosforth 'Wings for Victory' week was inaugurated.

16 May 1640
Lord Conway, the Royalist Commander has a mutineer shot in the Bigg Market.

18 May 1964
Eric Burdon and the Animals recorded 'House of the Rising Sun'.

20 May 1962
The film *Payroll* was released.

22 May 1940
The decision was taken to cancel Race Week Fair.

28 May 1942
Whickham View School opened, the first elementary school in the country to have a swimming baths on the premises.

5 June 1862
Geordie Ridley first sang 'Blaydon Races' at Balmbra's Music Hall.

9 June 2007
Comedy duo Ant & Dec first hosted *Britain's Got Talent*.

18 June 1941
The king and queen toured Tyneside and visited shipyards and armament factories.

21 June 1940
The Newcastle Voluntary Training Corps was formed.

23 June 1945
The Race Week festival opened.

26 June 1740
The 'One Day Rebellion' took place, as Keelmen and others stormed the Guildhall and appropriated the civic funds.

2 July 1940
A major air raid took place in the late afternoon. In Newcastle and Jarrow 13 people were killed, 123 were injured, and Spillers factory was hit in an attempt to destroy the High Level Bridge.

6 July 2004
BBC first aired *55 Degrees North*.

7 July 1940
A second evacuation scheme was inaugurated: 4,300 schoolchildren left by train.

8 July 1764
Stewart the pawnbroker shot and killed Robert Lindsay and was subsequently hanged on Town Moor.

10 July 1906
The King Edward VIII Bridge was opened.

12 July 1164
William the Lion, King of Scotland, was captured at Alnwick and imprisoned in Newcastle after raiding deep into Northumberland and murdering the inhabitants of Warkworth.

16 July 1945
German submarine U776 visited Newcastle Quayside.

17 July 1876
The Swing Bridge was opened.

17 July 1941
Princess Royal visited the headquarters of Northumberland and Durham War Needs Fund.

18 July 1940
High explosive bombs were dropped – 3 people were killed, many injured and considerable damage was inflicted including a hit on Heaton Secondary School.

19 July 1333
The Mayor of Newcastle and 300 militia were allegedly killed at the Battle of Halidon Hill, fighting against the Scots.

25 July 1941
Grey's Monument was struck by lightning and the head of statue destroyed.

27 July 1935
The first Newcastle Airport opened.

27 July 1993
Death of T. Dan Smith (born 1915).

29 July1941
Gracie Fields visited Tyneside to entertain war workers.

2 August 1894
Launch of *Turbinia* designed by C.A. Parsons.

7 August 1758
Sixty-eight-year-old Alice Williamson was hanged for burglary.

11 August 1980
Newcastle Metro commenced passenger services.

15 August 1940
There was a mass attack on Tyneside in the middle of the day: north-east fighter squadrons brought down 25 bombers without any losses to themselves.

15 August 1945
The proclamation of the end of the war was read by the Lord Mayor inSt Nicholas' Square. He lit a 100-ton bonfire on Cowhill.

16 August 1941
A spectacular wartime procession of units of the Services and their modern equipment took place.

19 August 1388
The date of the Battle of Otterburn – Percy sought revenge for the loss of his pennon but was defeated and captured.

19 August 1754
Dorothy Catinby was hanged for killing her illegitimate offspring.

20 August 1940
The Spitfire Fund was inaugurated to provide a Spitfire or Hurricane, the plane to be called *Newcastle upon Tyne*.

21 August 1650
Fifteen people were hanged on the Town Moor for alleged witchcraft.

21 August 1752
Richard Brown, keelman, was hanged for murdering his daughter.

21 August 1776
Andrew Mackenzie, a former redcoat, was hanged for being a highwayman.

26 August 1945
A 100,000 strong crowd watched a victory parade.

28 August 1944
First large-scale lifting of coal from the open-cast seam on Town Moor took place.

29 August 1850
Queen Victoria opened the new Central station.

1 September 1939
The first batch of 31,222 children from Newcastle schools were evacuated.

1 September 1941

An air raid took place from 10.00 p.m. to midnight. 100 bombs fell on Shieldfield, Jesmond, Byker, St Peter's, Walker and New Bridge Street goods station. The latter burned for a week. 50 were killed, 71 seriously injured, 140 slightly injured and an estimated 1,000 people were made homeless.

2 September 1939

A further batch of 12,818 mothers and children under school age were evacuated.

9 September 1513

The date of the Battle of Flodden. The English army, mustered at Newcastle, defeated the Scots and King James IV of Scotland was killed.

12 September 1942

A native of Newcastle, Private A.H. Wakenshaw (aged twenty-eight) of the 9th Battalion, the Durham Light Infantry, was posthumously awarded the VC for conspicuous gallantry.

13–16 September 1940

Relatively minor air raids occurred in the Heaton area.

17 September 2001

The Millennium Bridge was opened over the Tyne, making it the newest Tyne bridge.

18 September 1942

Horse-drawn cabs reappeared in the city, owing to the wartime petrol shortage.

19 September 1939

North Mail amalgamated with *Newcastle Journal* because of war conditions.

20 September 1906

The launch took place of RMS *Mauretania*, built by Swan Hunter.

26 September 1939
The Lord Mayor's War Needs Fund was inaugurated.

1 October 1861
The murder of Mark Frater by George Clark took place in Blackett Street.

3 October 1944
Royal Grammar School returned from evacuation in Penrith.

6 October 1854
The Great Fire devastated Gateshead and Newcastle Quaysides.

8 October 1940
Newcastle's Communal Feeding Scheme was inaugurated. It was intended that the scheme would form the basis of the distribution of free meals to people made homeless by air raid action.

14 October 1986
The Metro Centre retail complex opened.

17 October 1746
The Battle of Neville's Cross took place and King David II of Scotland was captured.

17 October 1939
There was an air-raid warning on Tyneside for 90 minutes – but no enemy action.

20 October 1644
The Scottish armies stormed Newcastle in the cause of Parliament, ending the siege and capturing both town and castle.

26 October 1942
General de Gaulle visited Newcastle.

2 November 1822
The *Tom and Jerry* attempts to run the Keelmen's blockade during the general strike of 'long stop' of that year.

2 November 1943
Stalingrad Sword of Heroism was on view at Laing Art Gallery.

7 November 1941
The prime minister (Mr Winston Churchill) paid a surprise visit to Tyneside and visited bombed areas and industrial concerns.

8 November 1989
Byker Grove first aired.

13 November 1093
King Malcolm II of Scotland (Shakespeare's Malcolm Canmore) is killed in battle at Alnwick.

14 November 1968
King Olav V of Norway opened the new Civic Centre.

15 November 1942
After being silent for two years, church bells were allowed to be rung to signal the British victory in the Battle of El Alamein.

17 November 1771
The Great Flood of Newcastle happened.

20 November 1939
A canteen for service men and women opened on Platform 8 at Central station.

26 November 1939
A lecture by John Gielgud entitled 'Shakespeare in Peace and War' was held at Theatre Royal, in aid of the Lord Mayor's Red Cross Fund.

30 November 2002
Cheryl Cole, as a member of Girls Aloud, won *Popstars the Rivals* beginning her show business career.

1 December 1939
There was an inspection of Civil Defence and ARP arrangements.

3 December 1944
The final parade of the Home Guard took place, following the 'stand-down' order 8 May 1945.

5 December 1942
Newcastle became the first port in the country to provide a rest centre for Dutch seamen.

7 December 1733
The strange affair of the 'Flying Donkey'.

7 December 1838
The Savings Bank Murder rook place.

18 December 1939
Newcastle War Savings Campaign was inaugurated.

29 December 1941
An air raid took place between 8.00 and 9.00 p.m. 10 bombs fell on the Holderness Road, Byker, Matthew Bank areas. 9 were killed, 16 seriously injured and 64 slightly injured.

BIBLIOGRAPHY

The authors have also consulted a number of excellent secondary sources including:

Armstrong, P., *Dark Tales of Old Newcastle*, Bridge Studios, Newcastle, 1990

Hepple, L.W., *A History of Northumberland and Newcastle upon Tyne*, Phillimore, Chichester, 1976

Middlebrook, S., *Newcastle upon Tyne, its Growth and Achievement*, Newcastle Chronicle & Journal, Newcastle upon Tyne, 1950

Moffat, A., & Rose, G., *Tyneside; a History of Newcastle and Gateshead from Earliest Times*, Mainstream, Edinburgh, 2009

Morgan, A., *A Fine and Private Place, Jesmond Old Cemetery*, Tyne Bridge, Newcastle upon Tyne, 2004

Pevsner, N., *The Buildings of England: Northumberland*, Penguin, London, 1992

Those wishing to explore Newcastle's role in the slave trade during the eighteenth century should refer to John Charlton's *Hidden Chains – the Slavery Business and North East England 1600–1865* (Tynebridge, Newcastle, 2008).

The authors have, wherever possible, attempted to acknowledge copyright material and, where they may have failed to do so is the result solely of oversight, any errors or admissions will be rectified upon notice. For all other errors the authors remain responsible.